A DECENT MEAL

A Decent Meal

BUILDING EMPATHY IN A
DIVIDED AMERICA

Michael Carolan

Redwood Press
STANFORD, CALIFORNIA

STANFORD UNIVERSITY PRESS
Stanford, California

© 2021 by the Board of Trustees of the Leland Stanford Junior University.
All rights reserved.

Printed in the United States of America on acid-free, archival-quality paper

Library of Congress Cataloging-in-Publication Data

Names: Carolan, Michael S., author.

Title: A decent meal : building empathy in a divided America /
    Michael Carolan.

Description: Stanford, California : Redwood Press, 2021. | Includes
    bibliographical references and index.

Identifiers: LCCN 2021018472 (print) | LCCN 2021018473 (ebook) |
    ISBN 9781503613287 (cloth) | ISBN 9781503629547 (epub)

Subjects: LCSH: Empathy—Social aspects—United States. | Attitude
    change—United States—Experiments. | Social groups—United
    States—Psychological aspects. | Right and left (Political science)—
    United States. | Attitude (Psychology)—United States. | Social
    psychology—United States. | Public opinion—United States.

Classification: LCC BF575.E55 C357 2021 (print) | LCC BF575.E55 (ebook)
    | DDC 152.4/1--dc23

LC record available at https://lccn.loc.gov/2021018472

LC ebook record available at https://lccn.loc.gov/2021018473

Cover design: Michel Vrana

Cover image: iStock (composite)

Text design: Kevin Barrett Kane

Typeset at Stanford University Press in 11/15 Arno Pro

Contents

A Decent Meal

CHAPTER 1

Journeys to the Heartland

T his book's origin story involves strawberries—what I've come to call the strawberry study.[1] A dozen individuals were recruited from middle-class and higher economic backgrounds from northern Colorado. The stated purpose of this exploratory study was to better understand what information participants absorbed about strawberry production—from facts to feelings—and whether this knowledge had any effect on their attitudes about industrial strawberries and the invisible labor that supplies eaters with this delicate fruit. I was especially interested in whether these outcomes varied depending on the knowledge-delivery method. Participants were first *told* about the processes and people involved through handouts and a documentary about immigrant strawberry laborers. Later, they *experienced* it by picking. They were also asked to use their phones to take photos while in the field.

The images were the biggest surprise, lending unexpected empirical weight to the qualitative interview data. They changed substantially over the course of the day. Morning frames were remarkable in their repetitive sameness—landscape shots broken up with the occasional arm's-length selfie. Yet by afternoon, with the sun hot overhead, the images told a different story. Selfies were closer, suggesting that the focal point was not the face but the exhaustion. Sweaty faces and wet, matted heads of hair. Upturned baseball caps showing sweat-drenched bills. A pair of soil-stained bare knees. A half-dozen pictures of trays held by fingers caked with dirt. By day's end, everyone—*everyone*—had taken photos that not only documented their physical exertion but accentuated it.

A week later, after bodies had had time to heal and minds the opportunity to reflect, I met with each participant. What I heard verified what the photos had shown me. One individual, Nick, had commented at the beginning of the study that "illegal aliens are stealing our jobs." "A bleeding-heart liberal" is not a term that has ever been applied to Nick; certainly, he would not see himself as one—*Thank Christ!* I'm sure he would add. He affiliates with a political tribe that watches Fox News religiously, prime-time Fox specifically. Yet, by the study's end, Nick's tone toward immigrants had changed.

Asked to reflect on his time in the field picking, he said, "Yeah, that probably isn't a job many Americans would want." He then took a long breath and exhaled. The air rushed between his teeth and made a whistling sound, buying him time to think, either about the actual answer or about the one he wanted to give. "Maybe we do need immigrants for some things; maybe I can be too harsh." Granted, Nick's growth as an empathetic individual toward this group is far from complete; after all, immigrants are here for much more than just manual labor. But if this pivot represents the beginning of something more, then I welcome it.

What is remarkable about Nick's response is not so much the content of his words but what they represent, and what that might imply about society on a much larger scale. Nick lacked empathy for agricultural workers (especially foreign-born ones), and this experience created a space within him for it. Empathy, I've found, starts not by changing minds but by changing our opinions of others. As for how those opinions get changed, you might be surprised by what I found.

Palms turned up and raised off the table, Nick's apologetic repose was not unique to the group; many described similar attitudinal shifts after exposure to that fieldwork. And they did this without ever meeting a single immigrant laborer. I am not saying the experiment changed their political loyalties, that it somehow changed their cognitive filters. By study's end they remained motivated partisans, just a little less so when it came to issues of immigration and immigrant labor.

I was reluctant to draw too many conclusions from this study. It was exploratory, after all. Without getting very specific, *something* had happened to those participants. Wanting to learn more, I set out from there.

We All Have a Duane Story

His skills as an arborist were put to work on a blustery winter day in 2017. Surrounded by peach trees and a couple dozen men from Mexico, Duane pruned as I chatted with one of the farm's owners.[2] It was mid-February. We were at a fruit orchard in western Colorado. Duane was providing research assistance—his Spanish was better than mine. We were investigating how federal immigration policies had impacted the state's fruit farms, a project that included interviewing some of those workers for whom the United States is a foreign land.

Though it was early afternoon, the winter sun hung low in the horizon. The skeletal trees looked as though they were decorated with flickering lights, such was the effect when the pruners' lopping shears caught the midday rays and glinted brightly. Duane looked remarkably at ease, not just with the shears but with those he was working alongside. He had teamed up with another gentleman. Standing shoulder to shoulder, the exhaust of their breath in the cold air mixed between their almost-touching baseball-cap bills. Even at 100 yards, I could make out bits of Spanish: . . . *aquí*. . . ; . . . *más bajo*. . . ; . . . *está bien* . . . The cold air and gentle breeze proved an especially good conduit for their laughter. It registered as if they were standing directly in front of me.

The next day, Duane was behind the wheel, driving an under-powered four-cylinder Ford Ranger over the 7,834-foot Raton Pass on the Colorado–New Mexico border. I was seated at the other end of the tattered bench seat. We were leaving the state to continue the research that had taken us to that western Colorado fruit farm. It was then that he shared with me some of his biography, which put into context the interaction that I just described.

Before attending college, Duane had been a hired hand on a farm. Best friends with the son of a large-scale fruit-and-vegetable grower in Washington State, Duane had been put on the payroll by the farmer as a favor to his son—those skills as an arborist the result of on-the-job training. Duane eventually proved his worth as a "gear head"; he was a prodigy when it came to small-engine repair.

Physically, Duane was a pretty nondescript guy. Being of what I consider average height and weight—about five feet, nine inches and 180 pounds—his brown hair had that just-got-out-of-bed look without appearing disheveled. This averageness stood in sharp contrast to his voice. He sounded like the baritone in a barbershop quartet.

Reflecting on his recent experience pruning, he remarked, "Seeing those immigrants, that brought back memories."

He admitted to being "a little racist" as a teen. I'm not sure that particular noun can be modified, but those were the words he used. Those sentiments extended to non-English-speaking immigrants. "I can't tell you how many times I got in trouble for arguing with my high school Spanish teacher," he confessed, adding, "I didn't need to learn another language, I thought. Immigrants should have been the ones learning a new language: English."

Events from that day working alongside Mateo—the other half of the aforementioned pruning team—stirred something within my thirty-year-old, white, middle-class companion: self-reflection. "I'm not *that* person anymore," he intoned.

"My parents would tell me repeatedly that I was wrong, and show me, show me data in some cases, which would refute my ignorance, like how I thought immigrants don't pay taxes or that they committed crimes at higher rates than other groups."

"What changed?" I asked.

Duane scratched the top of his head with the hand that had been resting on the manual stick shift before answering.

"Farmwork is all about getting into a rhythm. Focusing on the task at hand lends itself to forgetting who you're working alongside. You begin treating them, and they you, like a human being."

He glanced in my direction. "I guess my attitudes about immigrants changed after I got to experience them as fellow humans, during those moments when the baggage of our social and political allegiances is not so immediate."

Duane's parents repeatedly told him that his biases were unfounded and presented him with facts to support their position. Yet it took being put into a situation where he got to know this group as fellow humans. This stands in contrast to what usually happens when confronting someone different—an almost-reflexive need to assign people into political (Republican/Democrat, national/immigrant, etc.) and value-laden (e.g., friend/enemy) categories. The farmwork was disarming in that sense, a point he described in terms of it affording a rhythm. The migrants he got to know while tinkering with engines did not have brown skin but bodies that bled red and that hugged and held family members, just as Duane did, bodies that *faced* threats instead of representing them.

You probably know someone like this, someone who viewed a group through a narrow lens until, thanks to a series of transformational experiences, a lot more became visible. This book describes individuals like this, people who underwent a transformation. But rather than the result of happenstance, the experiences described were intentional, like in the strawberry study. You will be introduced to people who started at one place, entered into a meaningful experience, and came out with a more encompassing and empathetic view of others. The conclusion I keep coming back to is that facts alone cannot heal today's caustic political environment. We therefore need to rethink what I call the headland model of social change.

A body of land battered by waves of factual information is not impervious to change. But most of these alterations are matters measured in degrees—*inches* lost to erosion and the like. Changes of kind, of substance, are rare. Headlands do not change by nature of their experiences as headlands.

A Decent Meal gives voice to what we learn that cannot be easily reduced to words or statistics: the experience itself—the *heartland*. The project described is about amending the soil of our existence, creating encounters and experiences that afford new ways of living, feeling, and knowing. My use of the term *heartland* is not meant as a geographic reference. (In addition to the title of a popular Canadian drama series, available on Netflix, the heartland is commonly associated in the US with the Midwest.) Instead, the metaphor helps me describe a fissure in how Western thought has traditionally broken down experience. One way focuses on the head, cognition, and reason. The other, what I am calling the heartland, is a catchall for everything else, where you find such phenomena as emotion, embodiment, and affect—not that heart and head are actually separate, but we'll get to that later.

This book is testament to why the heartland matters and, more than that, how it just might be key to saving modern democracies.

The Headland Model: Faith Misplaced

My experiences as an educator have been sobering. It has not reached the level of an existential crisis, but it is close. Etymologically, a professor is someone who professes—to make declarations that, I used to think, advanced the human condition or at least got people to reevaluate attitudes and behaviors. How foolish to think that telling people facts will elicit changes in how they think and act.[3] Long gone are the starry-eyed days of thinking that minds and actions of the next generation can be fundamentally changed by my fact-based lectures.

What data will change the mind of a bigot or a xenophobe? If you think Donald Trump supporters are a basket of deplorables, what could I possibly tell you to make you feel otherwise?[4] Part of the problem with the headland model is that it overlooks the overwhelming empirical evidence concerning how cultural and political beliefs filter the facts we choose to see and acknowledge.[5] Traditional liberal political theories continue to advance the idea that good old-fashioned, well-reasoned talk holds the potential to solve any social ill.[6] How can that be if we hear only what we want?

We have a term for this: *motivated reasoning*.[7] Rather than using facts to objectively arrive at a political decision—or *any* decision, really—this framework argues that we rationalize our way into the decisions we originally wanted to make. This occurs thanks to both confirmation bias, a tendency to look only for information we agree with, and disconfirmation bias, which involves systematically dismissing information that we disagree with.[8] These biases are also especially strongly correlated with partisanship. This explains the tendency to reduce debates to being about the Left vs. the Right, whether talking about climate change, COVID-19, mask wearing, or whether Black lives matter.[9] The more we identify with a political party, the more we work to find ways to have our beliefs confirmed.

In 2018, Bell County High School student and valedictorian Ben Bowling gave the commencement speech. Nearly 80 percent of the county, located in southern Kentucky, voted for Trump in the 2016 presidential election.

"This is the part of my speech where I share some inspirational quotes I found on Google," Bowling is reported as saying. "'Don't just get involved. Fight for your seat at the table. Better yet, fight for a seat at the head of the table.'—Donald J. Trump."

The crowd erupted in applause.

Before the commotion had a chance to subside, Bowling cut in. "Just kidding," he said, adding, "That was Barack Obama."

According to the 18-year-old, the crowd quickly went quiet.[10]

The headland model for understanding attitudes and behaviors would have you believe facts speak to us like numbers in an equation, where "4+4" is to "8" like "exposure to similar information" is to "consensus." That is not the scenario described by young Mr. Bowling. The audience did not judge the merits of the quote by the principles it espoused but by who allegedly said it. I am not saying facts no longer matter, though that would make for a fitting refrain in this so-called age of alternative facts.[11] Facts are important, just not in the way they are conventionally portrayed by the headland model.

In one study, authors analyzed climate change survey data from three populations: the US public, scientists actively publishing on energy technologies, and congressional policy advisers. Its findings uncovered "evidence that the ideological divide about global warming gets significantly larger according to respondents' knowledge about politics, energy, and science."[12] More knowledge, in other words, was shown to *increase* the divide between climate change skeptics and those believing it to be real and human induced.

Strategies forward need to be informed by these realizations. You will read about experiences that touched participants so deeply that some of those cognitive filters changed. But I show how, in other instances, partisan-motivated reasoning was leveraged to enroll participation of the very individuals you would expect to be least interested in fostering empathy toward historically marginal groups. Yet, once enrolled, these hardheaded individuals reported a change of heart. Some experiments described even provide clues about when facts are more likely to matter, but only after individuals were primed by heartland encounters.

The Heartland Model: Closing Distances

Let us not forget that people in opposing political groups generally do not like each other.[13] And if federal hate crime statistics are any indication—the Bureau of Justice Statistics reports roughly 250,000 annually[14]—many in these groups hate one another. If you hate or even mildly dislike those who do not share your social and political affiliations, what are our options to moderate those biases and filters in the hope of providing a fighting chance for healing?

I propose that our search for possibilities can be aided by the idea of proximity.

When groups live physically, socially, and emotionally separate lives, they are far less likely to empathize with each other.[15] In this environment, stereotypes rule the day.[16]

Take society's evolving attitudes toward LGBTQ communities. More than two-thirds of US adults think gay marriage should be legally recognized. Back in 1996, that figure was 27 percent.[17] One thing that has been particularly helpful in moving the attitudinal needle: the reduction of social, emotional, and geographic distance. Nearly nine-in-ten US adults now say they know and regularly interact with someone who is gay or lesbian.[18] We have all heard stories of religiously conservative politicians undergoing a change of heart after the "coming out" of a loved one.[19] That empathy can overpower religious dogma speaks volumes to its political potential.

I am not talking about geographic proximity. The proximity we need to mitigate against hate cannot just be measured in inches or feet. Something else has to happen, too, as evidenced by recent demographic happenings, where diverse groups, whether they like it or not, are finding themselves living, working, studying, worshipping, and shopping within the same zip code, if not closer. There was a strong correlation between support for Trump throughout his presidency and a community's growing Latino population. White Democrats who previously backed Obama were among those included in Trump's base.[20] This aligns with other research detecting a positive relationship between recent Hispanic immigration and state-level variation in anti-Hispanic hate crimes.[21] Is this that kumbaya moment we think results from bringing different people physically together without attention to how these groups feel about each other? This physical closeness might instead be correlated with white nationalism and xenophobia. This is where strategies to reduce social and emotional distances come into the picture— approaches that promote connecting with others on affective ("I can feel his pain") and social ("She's not so different from me") levels.

My reference to the *heart*land is to nudge our focus beyond the unsubstantiated belief that facts alone will bring us together. Being told you're wrong and why. When does that ever work?

Total Eclipse of the Heart

As I work to identify what those heartland phenomena are, let me start by highlighting a distinction made by social psychologists and political scientists between values and attitudes. The former refers to the deep beliefs we all have about how the world is and ought to be, whereas the latter speaks to what we think about particular worldly aspects. Values are incredibly sticky, hard to change. Values help explain what gets filtered, while attitudes are among those outlooks that emerge from the process. A series of experiments has shown that tailoring advocacy to a person's values can shift attitudes toward a policy.[22]

In one study involving self-identified liberals and conservatives, the latter's attitudes shifted dramatically in the pro-environmental direction after exposure to what the authors called a "binding moral frame," where protecting the environment was portrayed as a matter of obeying authority, defending nature's purity, and advancing American patriotism. This exposure included having participants read statements like, "Show you love your country by joining the fight to protect the purity of America's natural environment," which spoke to conservatives' values more than the frames directed at, say, righting environmental injustices.[23] This pro-environmental shift in attitudes was especially apparent when the binding message was perceived as coming from an in-group.[24]

The power of in-group identification. Sound familiar? It should. Value-motivated cognition is not a reasoning deficiency but a reasoning adaptation directed at promoting the interest that individuals have in wanting to be part of a larger group.[25]

While interesting, this literature leaves me unsatisfied. Where do these deeper values come from, and how might they be changed? I am also not convinced that the solution to our current incivility and hate—the dissolution or ripping of the American fabric into factions—is better messaging. It feels like a superficial and insincere response considering the level of healing needed.

All of this brings me back to the origins of this book. This dissatisfaction, coupled with a few pivotal observations about proximity, germinated into an idea, which led to one exploratory study after another, until—well, now I have a book's worth of data. I suggest looking for solutions in actions rather than in solely the transmission of facts, which entails reevaluating the value of what we *do* and *with whom*. The conclusions add an important twist to how we think about how people perceive and respond to the world around them.

Why Food?

We all eat. No matter your political allegiances, spiritual beliefs, legal residency status, gender identity, or sexual orientation, food is your intimate. And like the other intimates in your life, there is a desire to know it, well, intimately.

Recently, I spent an entire weekend trying to learn how to make kolaches; there's something you have to do, over and over again, if you want to know it well. Our individual cultural heritage, what our ancestors *did*, is arguably connected with numerous activities—sewing, knitting, soap and candle making, tanning hides, gunsmithing. Yet food-related practices hold a special place in our hearts, as evidenced by the growing interest in heritage food. This includes not wanting a family recipe to die with one's grandparents, as in my case with kolaches. Grandma also knew how to make buttons from clam shells caught in local rivers. No one bothered to learn that aspect of my family's heritage. That knowledge died with her, even though the Heritage Crafts Association included button making as one of its endangered crafts.[26]

We might not know a lot about matters relating to food—we've all read statistics revealing the belief among some eaters that, for instance, milk comes from wheat[27]—but at least we are curious. While more than 70 percent of Americans say they know nothing or very little about farming or ranching,[28] more than half report taking steps over the last year to learn more about where their food comes from.[29] Perhaps that curiosity links to wanting to live a more environmentally sustainable lifestyle. A 2018 survey of 1,009 Americans, ages 18 to 80, found that 60 percent of participants considered it important that the food they purchase or consume is produced in a sustainable manner.[30] This helps explain why the late 20th-century Food from Nowhere regime is undergoing a transformation, as evidenced by enormous investments in the tracking and tracing of food for purposes of food safety, not to mention how this helps food firms minimize the potential for bad publicity, liability, and recalls.[31] Or take the growing interest in cooking, especially postpandemic. One pre-COVID survey found that more than 90 percent of US shoppers watch cooking shows.[32] More recently, a survey of more than 1,000 American adults conducted in early April 2020 had over half report cooking more (54 percent), and almost as many said they were baking more (46 percent) than before the pandemic,[33] a finding supported by some of my own research.[34]

Our inquisitiveness toward food seems to know no bounds, as the following chapters detail. Food is not a Red American or Blue American issue, just as it is not something that interests only the rich or poor. Household income may mediate what people eat,[35] yet wealth has nothing to do with one's dependence on a wonderment of food systems.

What if that inquisitive appetite could be used to engender something culturally healing in addition to more informed eaters?

Coming-to-Tables-and-More

We know from countless experiments that communication breaks down almost immediately when people with contrasting lived experiences are unwillingly brought together to hash out differences.[36] There is a reason why most families abide by the "No talk of politics or religion at the dinner table" rule: it's a conversation killer. But what if we changed the expressed purpose of the encounter? What happens when we are brought together not just to get along but also to learn more about our food systems? With that amendment, our response to others in the same space changes, often dramatically, as I illustrate through a variety of novel experiments.

This is not, however, one of those "come to the table" books. Commensality has been a long-studied and discussed topic in the food-studies tradition.[37] Another book on the topic would struggle to express anything that has not been written before. Besides, this book is really about what *precedes* those encounters. I am all for people eating together. But what about those who hate each other? The real work in that instance would be whatever got them to the table. Regardless of what transpires at most of these meals, getting them to agree to sharing the meal is itself a huge win.

I inserted the qualifier *most* into the previous sentence because of my chapter on wild-game dinners. Sometimes tables hold the potential to bring people together that would not otherwise knowingly share in the breaking of bread. What I found especially interesting about these events is how they disarmed participants enough to have honest, thoughtful discussions about a subject that usually starts with shouting and devolves further from there: guns.

What about those who cannot eat together? How are empathy and understanding afforded among those separated by great distances? How does sharing a meal or a hoe help resolve the bigotry and terror fueling the Darfur genocide? Political realities also have to be taken into consideration. And concerns over one's personal safety are important, too. No undocumented immigrant would ever willingly partake in a meal with designs to bring them to the table with a bunch of white nationalists.

The experiments discussed engage food in various ways, including self-proclaimed welfare warriors taking the SNAP (Supplemental Nutrition Assistance Program) Challenge, urban foodies detasseling corn on a large-scale conventional farm, white nationalists picking berries while mimicking certain conditions encountered by immigrant berry pickers, and deep-red Republicans gardening alongside progressive Democrats. Not only is this book about more than dinner tables; it includes practices other than eating.

It was surprisingly easy to enroll participants in these numerous food-related experiments. I doubt I would have had as easy a time convincing people to participate in other forms of cultural consumption, like had they been asked to participate in a foreign sport, watch Chinese Opera, or use a Serger sewing machine, like in a sweatshop. That would have felt to participants a strange ask, whereas the aforementioned activities involving food did not.

Food also has a long history of providing touchstones for everyday politics and symbolic boundaries. We know that attempts to position family meals as solutions to today's social ills place a disproportionate burden on working-class families and, in particular, mothers.[38] (Countless studies detail the discourses of "good mothering" and how strongly food ties into those societal pressures and performances.)[39] Just as food has the ability to bring people together and positively change attitudes, it is also used to push citizens apart—a way of signaling either approbation or disdain about others' choices. There is a level of judgment associated with food that does not exist for most other things we consume. And even that isn't consistent. There are more than a hundred recipes for deep-fried Twinkies on Pinterest—yes, they are now a thing in certain foodie circles. But when the dessert is eaten at a state fair by an overall-wearing midwesterner, it is often coded as lowbrow and gluttonous.

I am especially disheartened when food becomes weaponized, as it often does in welfare debates. For those who use what are colloquially called "food stamps" to *supplement* food purchasing activity, which is exactly what these benefits are supposed to do, what is wrong with people purchasing a treat once in a while? While middle-class families might be able to afford more than a bag of Cheetos to help their kids feel special, as sociologist Priya Fielding-Singh points out, "food serves as a symbolic antidote to a context of deprivation" among parents in low-socioeconomic households.[40] Put another way, inexpensive food (read: junk food) is often these parents' sole avenue for obliging their children's requests. Yet parents using food stamps to purchase, say, a cake—lest we forget that poor kids have birthdays, too—report getting the stink eye and receiving snide comments from judgmental cashiers and bystanders.[41] (Birthday cakes are eligible if nonfood decorations are less than 50 percent of the cake's value.) How food is being politicized, in other words, reflects broader sociopolitical trends. That is not to diminish its potential value for the task at hand. The points just made do not diminish food's unique ability to suspend some of the very judgments that it, at times, helps to amplify. The trick is to figure out how to take advantage of food's unifying qualities and to do so in a way that transcends the coming-to-the-table trope.

Why Now?

From a national poll taken in 2018: 69 percent of participants believe we have a major civility problem; 75 percent think our incivility is a crisis; 97 percent say it is important for the president to be civil.[42] Another national poll found that 90 percent believed it important for politicians to be civil to one another, a finding I find hard to square given that Trump garnered just under 47 percent (more than 74 million votes) of the popular vote in 2020. Being civil must not have been too important for some of that 90 percent.[43] The American Psychological Association cites the "current political climate" as a major stressor for its members' clients. Among Gen Z adults, 69 percent feel very or somewhat stressed about our national future, with 55 percent calling out specifically the political environment as a source of stress.[44] It is such a mess out there that I am reluctant to call what we are seeing "incivility," which seems tame—Mom and Dad fight, but this is something worse.[45] Look at what we are facing: mass shootings, some intentionally targeting immigrant communities; pipe bombs mailed to politicians; chants of "Send her back," directed at a Somali-born congresswoman; teens being physically assaulted for their choice of pro-Trump apparel; misogyny; sexism. The "why now?" question ought to be obvious.

One strategy growing in popularity for restoring civility to our politics is professionally facilitated conversations.[46] I have attended dozens, where people with divergent outlooks and political beliefs gather and talk things out. The problem with this solution is that the conversations are designed for those already willing to jump headlong into the uncertain. Inspiring stories come from these events, where self-proclaimed enemies become friends. But that only happens when both sides open themselves to the possibility.[47] And there's the rub: these events are aimed principally at tackling incivility among individuals who can already demonstrate a level of civility and respect to those confronted.

A 2019 report on the prevalence of hate speech in higher education surveyed equal-opportunity professionals from around the US, which generally meant those queried were employees of university diversity or student affairs offices. Of those surveyed, 82 percent *personally* encountered a hate crime.[48] In terms of types of hate-bias acts, about 64 percent of the professionals reported that in the prior two years, they encountered pamphlets with racist or Nazi symbols.

Twenty-two individuals—seven were Mexican nationals—were murdered in El Paso, Texas, on August 3, 2019, at the hands of a white nationalist. One in five teenagers in the US is bullied online.[49] In late 2019, a (now-former) high-school teacher in Waterloo, Iowa, threatened the then-16-year-old climate-change activist Greta Thunberg with a Facebook post that referenced his "sniper rifle."[50] In October 2020, an 80-year-old was killed after asking a fellow bar patron to wear a mask.[51] What are we to do about all this hate?

While it is important to provide spaces for people who are open to working through their differences, what about those who retreat further into their homogeneous in-group when faced with diversity and difference? You know the type: they see brown skin and think "illegal," their mind goes to "terrorist" at the sight of a turban, or they associate pickups and camo with terms like *bubba* and *gun nut*.

My optimism for these professionally facilitated conversations is further tempered by how they *look*. The demographics of those I have attended lean middle-class and slightly older, just who you would expect could take an afternoon or evening off for something like this. A bunch of white, middle-aged, well-to-do folks are learning to get along—great. It's a start, but only that.

What makes people want to participate in these events in the first place? That is the unasked question we need to be finding answers to.

To claim that empathy can be powerful and that it can bring about change is not new. The Bible is full of passages urging this kind of thinking: "So whatever you wish that others would do to you, do also to them" (Matthew 7:12); "If one member suffers, all suffer together; If one member is honored, all rejoice together" (1 Corinthians 12:26); "Remember those who are in prison, as though in prison with them, and those who are mistreated, since you also are in the body" (Hebrews 13:3). The idea of learning to walk a mile in another's shoes is not especially new either. Desegregation, Equal Employment Opportunity legislation, and the rise of reality television have in their own ways reduced the distances separating populations. Similarly, people like Barbara Ehrenreich—of *Nickel and Dimed* fame—have been trying for years to get us to understand how hard it is to be part of the working poor by talking about their own personal experiences temporarily living life in another's shoes.[52]

More than 100 years ago, however, such empathetic journeys inspired a revolution in the US and England. The revolution went by various names, most commonly known as American pragmatism or the settlement house movement.[53] For pragmatists (e.g., Dewey, James, Peirce), thinking is an iterative process whereby thought and action are inseparably connected.[54] Head and heart, in other words, are united. Settlement house activists, most notably Jane Addams, put this philosophy into action by having middle-class volunteers live and work alongside the tired, poor, and huddled masses. The movement espoused the power of physical proximity and social and emotional interconnectedness. For Addams, "sympathetic understanding" was a relational process that had both social and psychological dimensions, achieved through disruptive experiences (what she called "perplexities") that challenged traditional (read: xenophobic, classist, racist, etc.) values, attitudes, and beliefs.[55] This is all to say that a late 19th-century movement was founded on going to the "heartland" and increased public awareness of issues relating to the health, sanitation, and education of urban poor communities.[56]

Requiem for Partisans

While this book is political, I have tried to avoid making it partisan. We need to break from the politics of hate, fear, and exclusion that the Trumped-up corners of the Right so masterfully gin up and prey on. Yet I am equally frustrated with elements coming from the Left, their lack of empathy for rural America being especially infuriating. While my politics have leaned left for a long time, and I would gladly describe myself as a progressive were it not for others who already do, I am pretty disgusted with both parties right now. Neither Blue America nor Red America has a monopoly on empathy. Both are guilty of whipping up the flames that have set democratic institutions ablaze.

On the one hand, we know those on the Right are particularly attuned to in-group cues, causing many to be resistant to difference and dissonance.[57] Two factors have been identified as driving this position. One deals with the fact that the country is becoming more liberal—think same-sex marriage, marijuana laws, movements for universal health care, support for environmental regulations and gun control.[58] As political scientist Lilliana Mason explains, "With a generally left-leaning citizenry, Republicans do better by calling attention to identity differences, not policy differences, since the former allows them to connect more directly with the greatest number of voters."[59] This response is amplified by the fact that the party is especially homogeneous—the second factor.[60] This one-two punch has made some Republican voters worrisomely attuned to prompts suggesting that their in-group status and way of life are threatened and incentivizes party leaders to engage not around policy but at a level that indicates a country under "attack" (such as along the US-Mexico border) and that calls on (white) Americans to take "our" nation back.

On the other hand, the Left also has some explaining to do.

Jonathan Haidt, professor of ethical leadership at New York University's Stern School of Business, asked more than 2,000 respondents to fill out the Moral Foundations Questionnaire.[61] One-third were instructed to fill it out normally, answering as themselves, one-third were told to fill it out as a "typical liberal" would respond, and one-third filled it out as they thought a "typical conservative" would respond.

What did Haidt learn? That liberals had the most difficultly opening their minds. Wait—*what?*

Self-described liberals, especially those calling themselves "very liberal," were worse at predicting the moral judgments of moderates and conservatives than moderates and conservatives were at predicting the moral judgments of liberals. The takeaway: liberals on average do not understand conservatives. Haidt attributed this blind spot to the group being convinced of their rationality, open-mindedness, and enlightenment.

Or take the 2019 study published in *Socius,* a peer-reviewed journal published by the American Sociological Association. Based on the results of two internet-based survey experiments involving a total of 1,797 respondents, its authors write that a subset of liberals, not conservatives, are the group "most responsive to the implicit—and sometimes explicit—racial appeals of Donald Trump's presidential campaign."[62]

I found something similar after interviewing two groups: the first, 48 white Colorado residents, from rural and urban counties, who voted for Obama in either 2012 or 2008 before voting for Trump in 2016; the second, 28 Colorado residents of color, from rural and urban counties, who did not vote for Trump in 2016.[63] That aforementioned support among a subset of liberals toward implicit, dog whistle–type racial coding stems from, I believe, the strong norms of colorblindness in liberal political cultures. This is the idea that you are supposed to see the person and not the color of their skin, especially in a post–civil rights, post–Obama presidency era.[64] Colorblindness provides these Americans with discursive devices that can be used to defend the status quo by denying that racism persists while presenting outcomes in ways that are themselves colorblind. Examples of this include justifying residential and school segregation patterns as matters of individual choice; explaining education, employment, and incarceration inequities between whites and nonwhites as matters relating to differences in familial structure (e.g., single mothers vs. two-parent families) or culture; or opposing affirmative action on the grounds that it goes against the American principles of treating everyone the same.

Examples of colorblindness, while often subtle, abound. Democratic 2020 presidential candidate Pete Buttigieg made headlines in 2018 after video emerged, from 2011, of him explaining educational underperformance in "minority communities" by saying, "There isn't somebody they know personally who testifies to the value of education."[65] He was swiftly criticized, and rightly, for casting those education gaps as being about cultural deficits versus systematic racism.

This language works at multiple levels. We are horrible at talking about and engaging with difference. We have that small-*l* liberal ethos to thank for this, a political philosophy that celebrates merit and demands we treat everyone the same—that is, "We hold these truths to be self-evident, *that all men are created equal.*" So, at one level, even the well-intentioned risk repeating racist tropes without even knowing it thanks to this language. The other way colorblindness operates is by giving the not-so-well-intentioned cover, by providing those committing hate crimes an avenue to moderate and mainstream their language.

This book identifies strategies for nudging the electorate and the public—Red and Blue America and everyone else—in a direction that should help us heal as a nation and to do so in a way that celebrates difference. This means finding ways to equip citizens with the tools *to see* things like skin color, sexual orientation, and the like, which is the only way to take on systems of oppression working overtime to ensure that we *don't* see that stuff. In the face of this complexity, our collective response must be intentional and multifaceted. This book helps give that response direction, while offering people who are sick of it all a repertoire of options and a navigable path forward . . . into the heartland.

The Journey Ahead

While written for a general audience, this book is an example of unsettling scholarship, with *unsettling* serving as both verb and adjective. As the former, this is not conventional scholarship. Some will find my experimental sensibilities, as evidenced by the use of pre- and post-"exposure" exercises, as too contrived and perhaps a bit unsettling themselves—there is a long-standing debate as to whether social scientists should merely study the world or seek to change it. Others, meanwhile, will find the approaches taken as not experimental enough. Where's the control? The randomization? The double-blind element? Many of the usual signposts, and jargon, that academics use to mark their territory and amplify their identity as scholars are also intentionally disguised. I do this mainly to improve readability and make arguments more accessible. Some of the concepts and approaches with which I engage, without always calling them out explicitly, include affect theory, critical race theory, alterity and difference, extended mind, phenomenology, embodied cognitive psychology, and social identity theory.

At the same time, I want this book to unsettle *you*. Here, *unsettling* is an adjective in that it qualifies the noun *scholarship*. I hope you leave this book different from when you approached it; off-centered enough to approach problems in a different light and with new purpose. In truth, it is this latter meaning of *unsettling* that I most care about.

The next chapter gets right to work, describing the experiences of individuals who had attempted to put themselves behind the shopping cart of someone using SNAP benefits. I make a brief pivot in chapter 3, exploring questions around *why* we cannot get along. Phenomena interrogated include globalization, geographic sorting, the marketization of everyday life, and the fragmentation of media markets. The stories recounted lend weight to the argument that the problems are deep, meaning the responses must be collective, intentional, and multifaceted.

Chapter 4 gleans insights from a longitudinal qualitative research project, lasting from 2011 to 2018, involving individuals from a variety of different walks of life participating in community supported agriculture (CSA) platforms in Colorado. (The CSA model is a system connecting producers and consumers more closely by allowing the consumer to subscribe to the harvest of a certain farm or group of farms.) The experiences described occurred on CSAs where customers could volunteer on-farm labor in exchange for lower subscription rates, a practice with the potential to facilitate unique empathetic affordances. Chapter 5 recounts two experiments: in one, a group of right-leaning individuals, which included at least one white nationalist, picked berries; in the other, progressive urban foodies detasseled corn on a large-scale rural grain farm in Minnesota. The impact these experiences had on what participants thought they knew and felt about certain "Others" are discussed. In addition, evidence is provided that helps me to draw conclusions on how such physical encounters can be leveraged to mitigate the effects of motivated reasoning and other cognitive biases.

Chapters 6 and 7 continue with the review of food-related, empathy-evoking experiments. In particular, they highlight activities with the potential to repair a suite of divisions that cut especially deep: so-called rural-urban rifts. The experiences described in chapter 6 include the emergence of food-based supply chains that connect urban eaters and rural producers. Chapter 7, meanwhile, offers observations from wild-game dinners, where metropolitan, left-of-center foodies were brought into contact with Republican hunters from the countryside. It does not get more politically tribal in the US than when talking about guns.

The final chapter ties up loose ends and intentionally frays others. I also make appeals to broaden the conversation beyond food. Given my position as a professor and university administrator, I discuss, for example, the role higher education can play in mending some of these tensions. I remind readers, too, of the importance of critically unpacking what it means to say, "We have an incivility problem." On the one hand, incivility is so obvious because there is SOOO much animosity out there. But on the other hand, hate is not the same as boorish behavior. Killing 22 people at a Walmart in El Paso, Texas, is not commensurate with telling someone that they suck. I am also aware that the elite have long used the discourse of "incivility" to criticize dissent directed at the status quo.[66] Am I saying we should only be polite? Definitely not, but that is a subject for a later chapter.

Positionality: My Journey and Yours

While "I" make appearances throughout this book, it might be useful to establish my own positionality up front; after all, the book's key thesis is, to put matters simply, positionality matters. So: who is behind these journeys, and what did the journeys do to . . . me?

I am a white, heterosexual male. I am married with two kids. My day job: university professor and research administrator. I currently reside in Colorado but grew up in a small—350 people—town in rural Iowa. My politics have oscillated on the political spectrum between left-of-center to progressive left for more than 20 years, having volunteered for both Barack Obama and Bernie Sanders, though I started off calling myself a Republican. Heck, I caucused for Pat Buchanan in the 1996 Republican presidential primary!

Given my own journey, I feel like I know of what I speak. I attribute my transformation in significant part to countless encounters with socially othered groups who I had only known as a child through stereotypes and caricatures. This is not to suggest that my politics align with the Goldman Sachs–supporting wing of the Democratic Party. (I cannot believe how both parties handed out trillions in bailouts with little accountability, in response to the 2008 global financial crisis and again with the COVID-related CARES Act, passed in late March 2020.) Nor do I care for the haughty highbrow vibe occasionally wafting out of the Left toward those said to be clinging to their guns and "backward" beliefs.[67]

Was I changed by the encounters described in the following chapters? Lest we forget, I was there, too, for every experiment and interview. *Yes.* Whom "I" am today is not equivalent to whom "I was" a decade ago. And I have this research to thank for those opportunities for embodied-inspired reflection.

I have new friends—dozens, perhaps hundreds, from an almost unimaginable array of standpoints and political and social positionalities. The total experience also confirmed my belief that there are some truly despicable people in the world. For them, hope, I fear, is lost. But that segment of the population is not nearly as large as is often assumed. That is another insight I acquired while conducting the experiments recounted herein; people generally have the capacity to care for others not of their political tribe if given the opportunity to experience that difference firsthand.

I am also aware of the irony in writing a book *telling* readers about what we ought to be doing to foster an empathy-based revolution whose principal premise is that telling people does not do much to change minds and actions. I therefore try my best to *show* readers these journeys, hopefully to the point of unsettling complacencies and animating a change of heart.

Pandemic Partisanship and Social Distancing

It is late-2020. A few months ago, one in five people around the world was under lockdown.[68] While viruses are politically agnostic, how we perceive and respond to them has proven highly partisan as the world reels from coronavirus. With county-level Google Mobility Report data and individual cell phone data, scholars have already demonstrated how the activity of Americans during the COVID-19 pandemic is highly correlated with political party affiliation, with Democrats observing social distancing protocols at a far greater rate than Republicans, even after controlling for things like population density and local COVID cases and deaths.[69]

Meanwhile, masks have become a new flashpoint in the partisan culture wars. A study based on national polling data from more than 2,400 Americans noted that, after controlling for a range of potentially confounding variables, partisanship is a strong predictor of one's likelihood of wearing a mask.[70] Things are so bad that people are getting beat up and severely hurt—even killed—over these important facial accoutrements.[71]

A narrative has emerged on the Right that wearing a mask is a sign of weakness, whereas refusing to wear one demonstrates strength.[72] There has also been a tendency to lean on visual racist tropes to cover the COVID-19 outbreak, such as where Asians in masks have become the "face" of the coronavirus, most notably early in the outbreak.[73] It's "the China virus," remember.[74]

The crisis has also heightened the importance of our food supply and how fundamentally brittle those supply chains are. In April 2020, at the height of the global lockdown, prices paid to livestock and dairy farmers crashed while the retail cost of products like pork and milk skyrocketed. I know farmers in Iowa who were feeding their hogs a special ratio of meal designed specifically to keep them at the same weight, while euthanizing entire litters to keep herd and head numbers steady—many slaughterhouses had closed owing to outbreaks—while meat counters at nearby grocery stores were bare. COVID reminds us we need a food revolution as much as one rooted in empathy. Perhaps we can do things that have a positive impact on both fronts.

Lastly, what better time to have some grand political project designed to get people together. But as a sociologist, I know full well the power of routine and habit—remember, again, embodiments matter. Just as I know people who act as if COVID were the common cold, I know plenty of others who still live in fear of physical proximity. The latter group has not entered an establishment other than their grocery store for the last ten months—no restaurants, coffeeshops, gyms, stores. How will COVID impact our collective capacity to want to be with others who are different from us? Even with medical-grade protections, including face masks and rubber gloves, many today have a negative visceral reaction when their six-foot bubble is breached, even in some cases when that "other" is family. If there ever was a time for federal policy directed at increasing conviviality, that time is *now*.

CHAPTER 2

How Would You Stomach That?

I N THE WORDS OF Mark Twain, "Truth is stranger than fiction, but it is because Fiction is obliged to stick to possibilities; Truth isn't."[1] If I were to tell you a story about a fictional character named Ed, a gun-toting, right-wing, socially conservative Republican, who survived for a few weeks on food stamps to prove he could, but ended up rethinking his entire worldview—you would tell me, "Great, nice story. But things like that don't happen." Fair enough. I always try to gently encourage my students to *trust but verify*. Is it so remarkable to think an experience this basic holds transformative attributes? Now, were I to tell you that "Ed" is a pseudonym for not one person but many, and his marked change of heart had been recorded, you'd say you need the evidence.

I had students first do the SNAP—Supplemental Nutritional Assistance Program—challenge more than a decade ago. Social scientists are generally skeptical of the idea that someone could ever put themselves in the shoes of another, especially if that "someone" is a college student and the "other" someone is living in poverty.[2] Many critical scholars emphasize the importance of standpoint, the idea that one's social location, their experiences and biography, has to be taken into account when trying to understand their views of what is and what ought to be.[3] The position has a certain undeniable veracity to it. Who I am and what I think about the world has obviously been shaped by my experiences. If you have not had those experiences, who are you to say that you understand me?

Yet empathy is necessary for communities to come together, for society to operate. If you accept the evidence—*overwhelming* evidence, I might add—as to the limits of headland experiences in eliciting attitudinal and behavioral change, we can do one of two things. We can either collectively throw up our hands and quit caring, or we can point to the fact that people do change—like the alt-Right German politician who converted to Islam after spending time with Muslim immigrants[4] or the hardened cultural warriors who accept gay marriage after a loved one "came out"[5]—and learn from those experiences. Heck, maybe we can even try replicating them.

We all have our own standpoints. Could that be taken as a reminder that getting to know someone different from oneself involves work and time? And even then, any understanding and empathy achieved is incomplete. To say that because of our different standpoints we should not even try to put ourselves in another's shoes is to cede all hope that we can ever learn to care for and respect one another beyond the groups with whom we agree.

I first assigned the SNAP challenge on a whim. This was also back when I gave too much purchase to the headland model of behavioral and attitudinal change, thinking I could tell my students what it is like to live on food stamps and that they would get it. I therefore never expected to hear what I did from that population in the afterglow of a completed SNAP challenge. But then again, truth can be stranger than fiction.

SNAP: A Primer

SNAP is better known by its older name: food stamps. Beginning in 1939, the food stamp program began as the country was leaving the Great Depression behind and entering a multitheater world war. The program allowed those who qualified to buy orange-colored stamps equal to their normal food expenditures. For each dollar of orange stamps purchased, they would also receive 50 cents worth of blue stamps. The orange stamps could be used to purchase any food. Blue stamps, however, only bought food classified by Uncle Sam as surplus: the project was originally conceived as a response to overproduction and underconsumption. The program ended in 1943 because, to quote from a historical account of SNAP by the Food and Nutrition Service, "the conditions that brought the program into being—unmarketable food surpluses and widespread unemployment—no longer existed."[6]

The idea lay dormant until another pilot food stamp project was put into play from 1961 to 1964. The program was then made permanent with the passage of the 1964 Food Stamp Act. From the beginning, the program was a political hot potato, as no politician or party wanted to be seen holding it for too long out of a concern of getting burned. It has long been easier to score political points, regardless of political affiliation, by showing welfare recipients tough love. Or none at all.

Should we work diligently to eliminate false positives, in other words, eradicate those instances where someone is falsely identified as being eligible when they are not? Or should we cast a wide net, realizing that most people lack the time and expertise to fill out an elaborate application that would make a bureaucrat blush? I would rather see a program that is accessible, which catches as many of those in need as possible, even if that means risking that someone could take advantage of the system. Besides, we know that the vast, *vast*, VAST majority of government SNAP money is going to those who actually need it. To quote from a recent report by the USDA: "Our data show that only about 0.2 percent of SNAP benefits went in 2017 to households with monthly disposable incomes—net income after deducting certain expenses like high housing and child care costs—above the poverty line."[7] Yet some in government continue to call for huge cuts to SNAP to score political points.

One of these individuals was Rob Undersander, a Minnesota retiree who discovered that he could apply for and receive SNAP based on his income alone, without factoring in for assets. He immediately alerted the media after receiving his card in the mail and ultimately testified about his experiences before the Minnesota legislature and, later, the US House of Representatives. During his testimony he shared his financial reports. After factoring in his retirement investments, he was a millionaire.

The SNAP application process in Minnesota is typical. Most states consider income and do not inquire about personal assets or benefits from other government safety-net programs. The reason? Many people who genuinely need SNAP do not apply, either because they think they do not qualify or, more commonly, because they are ashamed that they do. Eliminating an asset check is supposed to encourage participation while reducing government cost—remember, this added level of oversight would not happen magically. Finally, and perhaps most important, such a policy encourages those eligible to have some personal savings—an incentive that can only be truly appreciated, I realize, if one possesses some degree of empathy toward this group.[8]

SNAP eligibility varies by state. In my state of Colorado, to give you a sense of the income levels we are talking about, a one-person household's annual income cannot exceed $16,237—add $6,000 for each additional person. (The average rent for an apartment where I live, Fort Collins, is $1,573 a month, which ought to put that income level into some perspective.)[9] You will be notified of your eligibility within 30 days of submitting your application. During that waiting period, applicants will complete an eligibility interview—conducted over the phone or in person—and give proof of any financial information provided. People can receive SNAP benefits within seven days if they meet additional requirements, such as if their household has less than $100 in liquid resources and $150 in monthly gross income, or if the household's combined monthly gross income and liquid resources are less than what is paid monthly for rent/mortgage and utilities.[10] Those who qualify receive an Electronic Benefit Transfer (EBT) card, which works like a debit card. Benefits are automatically transferred each month.

A woman called in to her local news station in Miami, Florida, in 2018, after attempting to help out someone in front of her in the checkout aisle. This person needed another $12 to pay for her items. Her SNAP card came up short. The clerk, however, refused to take the money, explaining, "That's why they have babies, so they're getting all the free stuff." The caller's daughter took to Facebook to vent about the encounter, writing, "My mom and I agree that this is exactly what is wrong with the world. Where is the compassion and basic human decency?"[11]

I might have an answer to that question.

Paul, a Lot of Students, and an Idea

He leaned on the end of the hoe, the business end resting flat against the ground. His large hands were supersized against the thin handle. Surprisingly, the skin looked papery thin, even delicate. The knuckle lines circled his fingers from nails to wrists. I was almost expecting to see blood, they cut so deep. And the veins reminded me of buried wire wrapped in blue insulation.

They were the hands of someone who had spent most of his life doing hard labor. Fifty-five years old, Paul had spent 37 of those years "building shit"—residential and commercial construction, mainly. That had stopped recently. He had been fired. I did not ask why, and he did not volunteer. When I met Paul, he was a month into his SNAP benefits.

I am starting here because, as I have come to tell this story, Paul plays a central role in its introduction. The SNAP challenge is something I had contemplated assigning to my students well before I actually did. Maybe my meeting with Paul was a trigger. Regardless, it conveniently sums up what I would expect to hear from someone who knew welfare only by way of headland experiences, by being told about it on CNN or Fox News or by what they read on the subject.

We were introduced by a mutual friend. I had been traveling around Colorado talking with residents outside the state's heavily populated Front Range—that area running down the middle of the state where the eastern plains meet the Rocky Mountains. Paul lived in a small town that was closer to Kansas than Denver. The interview took place at his house.

"Goddamn welfare." Head shaking, voice low, eyes focused on the hoe, he seemed to be talking to himself. His voice was a slow, southern drawl, hardened by years of smoking that sounded both half-asleep and angry. After a few seconds, the wood between his hands began to creak. The blue veins in his hands arched. Squeezing the handle, his trance held. Curious as to what he would say or do next, I waited. Not wanting to disrupt his train of thought, I casually ran my hoe through the same spot of ground, careful not to make any movements or sounds that might break his concentration.

"I'm the guy that believed people on welfare had it too good. Steak every night; ham and eggs for breakfast." His eyes went back to the hoe before he confessed, "I was wrong; I'll admit it. I believed a line peddled by rich blowhards who don't know the first thing about being unemployed." He would not name names, perhaps not wanting to betray his tribal allegiances any more than he already had. He was, however, a regular listener to partisan talk radio—I had heard Sean

Hannity playing on an unseen radio when Paul had greeted me at the door.

The hard part over, as Paul did not admit to being wrong often, his eyes locked on mine. "What's that saying about walking a mile in another's shoes?" he asked, adding, "That you can't know what another is going through until you've done it? Amen, brother."

He got me thinking.

The SNAP challenge (also known as the food stamp challenge) involves purchasing food using only the monetary equivalent of what one would receive if they qualified for the government benefit. The average monthly payment for one person is around $125, which means the "challenge" part centers on trying to eat healthily on about $4.20 a day.[12] If a person eats three meals a day, that translates to a little over a buck a meal.

I started making the exercise an assignment in one of my larger (100+ students) classes. The students, I thought, would find the exercise interesting. I never expected it to have the impact on as many as it did.

Students were asked to spend only $29.40 on food for one week and then write a reflection piece. More than 1,000 students have participated in this exercise. I also had them respond to the following four-part question (once before the challenge, and then again after its completion):

On a scale of one to 10 (1 = strongly disagree; 10 = strongly agree), how strongly do you agree with the following statements about SNAP?

1.   Benefits are generous and sufficient to eat well.

2.   The majority of recipients abuse these payments.

3.   Recipients have no right to complain about benefits.

4.   I believe recipients have used benefits to buy steak and lobster.

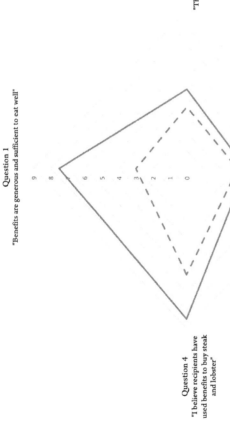

Question 1
"Benefits are generous and sufficient to eat well"

Question 2
"The majority of recipients abuse these payments"

Question 3
"Recipients have no right to complain about benefits"

Question 4
"I believe recipients have used benefits to buy steak and lobster"

Time 1
Time 2

FIGURE 2.1   Average scores for 1,000+ responses, pre- and postchallenge.

Figure 2.1, which goes by various names—spider chart, spider web, radar chart—depicts the average scores across all respondents for each of the four choices at both points in time. It is interesting that the average response to each of the four selections changed as much as they did in the span of roughly a week.

Whoever said women and men cannot live on bread alone never tried subsisting on a diet of generic canned tuna, Top Ramen, and dollar cheeseburgers from McDonald's—an extremely monotonous diet, to say nothing of its nutritional value. Many of the students talked about being surprised that eating on four dollars a day can be a real chore, and bore. Most had experienced days when money was tight. Yet, in the words of one, "a check from the Ps"—parents—"or my employer was never far away."

We can also see evidence that facts alone do not an attitude make. Take how students responded to the question, "I believe recipients have used benefits to buy steak and lobster." Most students reported hearing stories about food stamp abuse, which explains their responses to the question when first asked. The SNAP challenge did not present students with alternative data—which is to say, the experience did not confer upon them facts that refute the possibility of benefit improprieties. Yet it did "teach" them something that mitigated their feelings on the subject.

One student, whose answer to the question changed from a nine to a four, explained their change of heart this way:

"I think you have to experience eating on four bucks a day to realize those stories are wildly overexaggerated. I'm not saying it [it being fraud] doesn't happen. There's just no way it's as bad as the critics say it is. They might think it is. But that's only because they've never had to navigate through the experience."

The challenge was incorporated into a couple of years of classes. Each semester brought similar outcomes. With each, the itch to create a proper research experiment around the SNAP challenge grew.

Instead of students, for this project I sought individuals who considered *welfare* a dirty word and who stigmatized those on it. Could the SNAP challenge change their attitudes as well?

Starting a Dialogue

With the phone pressed against her ear, Martha looked up from one of the café booths and waved me forward while flashing a smile. "I'm a straight shooter. I'll tell you like it is, and I expect the same from you," she said into her oversized Samsung Galaxy. I had driven to this café on the Colorado eastern plains to meet with this county commissioner—an elected official who sets policy and budget for her county. Martha wore a black, belted pantsuit and talked the way I expected a self-assured community leader to talk.

We met at the café to review the exercise's ground rules and to have that first interview. Before I could slide in across from her, she shot a finger up and mouthed, *Just wait.* She ended the call seconds later and inched out from the seat in a hop-scoot motion that seemed to originate from her lower half. Standing erect, she reached out and shook my hand and bade me welcome, exchanging the usual pleasantries about my drive and if I had problems finding the place. I then followed her toward the back of the building, through one of those accordion walls that separate one room into two. Sealing the room off from the rest of the dining area, she took a seat and directed me to do the same.

Letting out a long breath, she slumped ever so slightly into the chair, displaying a confident ease. The private room. Her relaxed air. I was feeling good about this interview. Information conveyed during these exchanges are of little value if respondents feel on edge.

As this was part of a study, rather than an assignment, changes had been made to the student SNAP-challenge protocol. For one thing, participants were asked to take the challenge for two weeks, not one. Moreover, all participants were interviewed twice about their eating habits, as well as about their attitudes toward public assistance and the recipients of those benefits. One interview occurred prior to beginning the challenge; another happened after. Participants also had an assignment during the challenge. They were asked to use their smartphones to create an audio recording of their first and last shopping trips and of one "somewhere in between." Each was lent Bluetooth earbuds, which allowed them to carry out the tasks hands-free and less conspicuously. I was fishing with this ask, hoping to catch something interesting but not knowing exactly what that would look—or more accurately *sound*—like.

The project began with me calling acquaintances throughout Colorado—people I knew through previous research. I have been doing work in the state for decades, so this statewide network is extensive. Without much effort, I eventually signed up 22 adults to participate in the study (the $100 gift card offered at the start of the study to incentivize participation helped, I am sure).

Why would anyone agree to participate? I admit I had concerns that the experiment might have been a bust owing to a lack of participation. These fears, it turns out, were misplaced. Although people were not clamoring to participate, most of those who did participate were surprisingly agreeable to the prospect of giving the challenge a try. There were degrees of bravado expressed early on that helped to contextualize this willingness. One particularly boastful expression, from an elementary-school teacher—Sophia—went like this:

"Yeah, sure; count me in. I can do this. It will prove a point, that these handouts are plenty generous."

Remember what I said earlier, about how motivated reasoning represents not only a (headland) barrier but that it might also offer (heartland) opportunities. Participation in the challenge was not viewed as something that might threaten subjects' core political beliefs. And for some, it was even considered a vehicle to strengthen their tribal position.

The aim was never to establish a random sample. I had a good idea of where participants stood on the subjects of welfare and welfare recipients even before reaching out. In other words, I got the group that I wanted. Most leaned right politically, though four were registered as unaffiliated. Of the 22 who completed the challenge, 10 resided along the state's populous Front Range.[13] The remaining 12 lived in nonmetropolitan counties. Among the state's 64 counties, 24 have the "rural" designation and another 23 fall within the category of "frontier"; the latter refers to those with a population density of six or fewer persons per square mile. Six of those participating in the study came from frontier counties. Martha was one of them.

She was in her mid-50s. After putting in 20 years with the army, she moved to Colorado to be closer to her husband's aging parents. Since then, Martha had become active in state-level politics, volunteering for various Republican candidates. "They love my military background, the Republican Party, that is," she beamed. And I am sure the fact that being a woman, in a party that overwhelmingly elects males, did not hurt her political prospects either.

Being a government official, she admitted that the challenge would be a good experience, though there was some bluster there, too.

"I know I should say 'yes' because of my position. It might give me some insight that, as a public official, I ought to have." Then she smiled and said, "This will be good; it will give my words more weight when debating the role of government with colleagues from the other side of the aisle."

When discussing attitudes toward SNAP benefits and recipients, Martha's answers were in line with what one might expect to hear from a lifelong Republican. Unlike the others taking the challenge, Martha actually knew many of the nitty-gritty details—from what it takes to qualify, to benefit levels and eligible foods. When she spoke, her tone conveyed a level of certainty not always present at this stage of the exercise among other participants.

"Yeah, I'm ready to do this." I was not sure if it was excitement or defiance that I was picking up in her tone and posture. When asked to predict whether she would be able to complete the challenge, she scoffed. Her reaction didn't seem to be directed at me but at the premise that she was about to undertake something difficult. "You're looking at someone who was in the first Gulf War." Martha's unit supported supply lines during Desert Storm. "I think I can eat on a strict budget for 14 days."

Martha's Change of Heart

Two weeks later, we met at that same café. It was the first day after the challenge, as evidenced by the remnants of what had started as a whole Denver omelet and cinnamon roll on the table in front of her. "I was hungry!" she said between the final chews of roll. She gestured for me to take the seat opposite her. The Martha I interviewed still exuded confidence. But unlike before, that defiance had been replaced with an admission that the *challenge* designation is apropos.

The interview was insightful on a couple of levels. She did confess to "finding the challenge harder than expected." I will circle back to this point momentarily, as it is central to my argument. The point I want to unpack first, however, centers on how her privilege had crept into the experience. Her privilege, as a solidly middle-class professional, allowed for an indiscretion that created an opportunity for further reflection.

"It would have been a lot harder if I didn't have Costco." Trips to Costco are not in the spirit of the challenge, though I never explicitly forbade participants from shopping at this members-only warehouse. I discovered that she had traveled to Costco prior to the challenge, where she "loaded up"—her words. She stayed under the

$4.20 a day allocation by portioning out that haul, calculating cost on a per-meal basis.

While called the *Supplemental* Nutrition Assistance Program, for many recipients SNAP constitutes the total of their food budget. And that is only if they are lucky, as the benefit often only gets them as far as three out of the expected four weeks.[14] Loading up every now and again at a big-box discount store is thus not in the cards for many SNAP beneficiaries. When trying to eat on four dollars a day, buying "bulk" means purchasing two bananas instead of one.

The Costco in question was also roughly 100 miles away. A 200-mile roundtrip grocery run? That is not an option for the transportation insecure, who tend to also be SNAP recipients.

Access to reliable transportation is inversely correlated with household income. In other words, saving money on food by spending it on gas is a luxury that the poor cannot afford.[15] I debated whether to challenge participants to walk or use public transportation when making food purchases in order to replicate the transportation insecurity experienced by those in poverty. Yet such instructions would have reflected an urban bias, as public transportation options—for example, buses, light rail, even biking—do not exist for most rural residents. (Technically, biking is an option, but the distances involved make it an unrealistic one.) Of rural areas in the US, 20 percent have been classified as food deserts, meaning their residents have to drive considerable distances in order to eat.[16] To make matters worse, a higher proportion of the population in rural areas is mobility impaired, a status that includes being either physically disabled or lacking access to an automobile.[17] The situation is particularly acute among the rural elderly.[18]

Yet, Costco trip and all, Martha still found the exercise challenging.

"Some days were better than others," she confessed, dabbing the corners of her mouth with a napkin so as not to smudge her lipstick.

She went on to describe some of the main pain points of the exercise. All were familiar to me, having heard each, ad nauseam, from others after taking the challenge: too many carbs, not enough fiber, the monotony—there are only so many ways you can eat generic canned tuna, store-brand pasta, and frozen veggies on a tight budget.

When the subject turned to SNAP recipients, Martha waxed poetic as she reconciled her recent attitude changes with the positions espoused by the self-described welfare warriors whose campaign bumper stickers adorned her Chevy Silverado pickup.

"I'm not sure if it was actual hunger or the fact that you tend to think more about food when you don't have it. I hadn't thought *that* much about food since I was nursing my two boys." She leaned back in the booth, rolling her shoulders forward. The effect, whether intended or not, gave the impression of someone admitting defeat, or at least a rethink.

"In principle, handouts ultimately help no one. Liberty is not something that can be given, because that leads to dependence. That being said, my principles shouldn't blind me to what I just experienced. I can see the value of increasing the award amount. A few more dollars a day would make a huge difference. I doubt you would find a better return anywhere, where a few bucks could exponentially increase someone's well-being."

Her eyes held mine. It was not the look of someone lost in thought. She seemed, rather, to be gauging my reaction. Showing my best poker face, I returned her gaze. Whatever she saw in my face, it did not dissuade her from offering a poignant reflection: "Politicians are easily moved by principles, especially when they have no life experience to lean on. I'm not saying this [*this*: the challenge, I presume] is an elixir by any means. But it might just be what we need to start a dialogue."

Dissonance You Can Feel

"They-should-stop-complaining-and-get-a-job!" Terry growled behind his long white beard. I had asked if he empathized with SNAP recipients and whether he thought the four-dollar-a-day benefit was sufficient. The question must have really riled him. A fast talker by nature, when he was agitated, his words tended to jam together.

Terry lived in Denver. Recently retired, he had spent 30 years working in information technology for various firms in the area. Terry's daughter connected us. He was doing the challenge for her, whom Terry had described as "a good kid with misplaced priorities." Terry was registered as an Independent but described his principles as leaning libertarian. His daughter's affiliations, meanwhile, lay at the other end of the political spectrum, which is to say, she was a Democrat. His motivations for participation did concern me after he let slip that he was "doing this to blunt her argument that I have no clue what people on welfare go through." Then, his excitement growing, he added, "That isn't going to be true-much-longer!"

Terry's motives did get me wondering. What would the *right* reasons be for participating in such a challenge? If we expected people to come into these exercises wanting—*needing*—to change, what would that accomplish? This requirement might be laudable for participation in Alcoholics Anonymous, but I am writing this book based on the conviction that we cannot afford to wait for the world to magically wake up to the dangers of tribal politics. We need to act now, which means pressing forward even when participation is predicated on problematic motivations. When you think about it, the Terrys of the world—those who remain seemingly incapable of seeing beyond tribal identities—are exactly who we need to involve. Grounding this book on data collected from participants who wanted their minds changed would be less powerful. I was interested in people who left me guessing where they would land postchallenge.

I communicated with Terry multiple times prior to this meeting, over email and phone. During at least two of those exchanges, I told him what his daily food budget would be if he took the challenge. That did not stop him from making comments about using SNAP benefits to eat "steak and lobster." The first time the comment came out as, "I don't like lobster so you won't find me eating it"; later, he said, "Maybe I'll eat steak every day to make a point."

He knew what steak and lobster cost. To be sure, I asked. "At least ten bucks a pound," he answered. Yet, somehow, he thought these foods could be eaten with some regularity on a SNAP budget, an excellent illustration of how *telling* someone's facts—or providing numbers—is not always enough to change attitudes, not when one's cognitive filters will have none of it.

A few days after our first interview, Terry sent an email inviting me to access a Dropbox folder. There I found the audio file of his first shopping experience since beginning the challenge. The subject line of the email read, "I'm usually not this indecisive, really!"

His commentary was definitely colorful, but it took a couple of listens to piece together an image in my mind's eye. Later exchanges with Terry confirmed I had done a faithful job doing this.

The following comes from that audio file: "Christ, I'm not paying *that*, not when *this* is on sale. Bumble Bee it is! I can add salt." Helped by an image of the receipt, I was able to determine that this comment happened as he placed the sale-priced reduced sodium canned tuna in his basket.

Terry struggled to come within budget during that shopping trip. After considerable deliberation, his basket in the checkout line held milk, corn flakes, bread, cheese, sliced ham, tuna, mayonnaise, two bananas, and an apple. Talking out the math to himself, he put back the apple. Doing the math a second time, he reduced his basket further. He left the store with one fruit, a lone banana.

I had been anticipating my exit interview with Terry. The views he initially espoused were particularly pointed, denouncing government handouts of any form, almost always in an agitated flourish: "Goddamn-government-handouts!" Later, the audio files of him shopping offered a glimpse into how he might have been processing the challenge. In one file, Terry can be heard cussing out one especially inexpensive food item. Over an instrumental rendition of BTO's "Takin' Care of Business" playing on the store's speakers, he is caught saying, "No more fucking tuna; I'm growing gills." It was clear to me that the challenge was a source of frustration for him.

His final interview had to wait a little longer than we'd originally planned. Terry came down with a nasty cold during the last days of the challenge. This postponed things by almost a week. Fully recovered, he met me at a park a block from his house in Denver.

I mention his sickness because it made an appearance in our conversation that day in the park. After we had moved past the pleasantries, Terry volunteered that he "sort of cheated." Looking beyond my shoulder to the little league baseball game in the distance, he said, "I went overbudget both weeks; those last few days I really broke the bank."

It was at this point that the flu was referenced. "I was sick. I wanted some fruit and tea, some soup that wasn't just water and salt. The box of tea alone was over five bucks." He then mentioned the added budgetary squeeze inflicted by the over-the-counter medicine. "Even buying generic, that nighttime cough medicine, and ibuprofen and nasal spray; heck, it ate up damn-near an entire week's food budget, right there."

Terry talked of being "surprised" by the whole experience and used the interview to process what he was thinking. He had abandoned watching the ball game in the background and was now looking at me intently. While explaining that his core beliefs on government handouts remained—"I still don't like 'em"—he admitted that the challenge gave him a new perspective.

"What we think is based on what we know, and for some things we don't know a whole lot. We should all welcome an activity that gives us perspective," he said.

When imagining a unique or foreign experience, the best we can do is take something already known, or some amalgamation thereof, and build out. It is somewhat like attempting to explain to someone a new color. Try doing that without describing an already experienced hue. The SNAP exercise gave participants new experiences and sensations that then informed social situations previously too foreign to suitably grasp.

The little league game came to an end. Freshly freed, those in the stadium swarmed our area of the park. A horde of younger siblings and parents, forced to sit patiently through six innings, now had an outlet to release all that pent-up energy.

Forced to share our privacy with rambunctious families, we looked at each other and exchanged smiles. No words needed. We stood and started walking toward Terry's house. After some distance was placed between us and the commotion, I resumed the questioning. The first thing I asked had been in the back of my mind for a while, in part because I was never entirely pleased with how I was thinking to ask it.

Throwing caution to the wind, I inquired, "What surprised you most about those two weeks? Any insights from experience that you'd like to share—?"

Terry stopped in his tracks. A wave of doubt rushed over me: *Oh God, did that come out wrong?* But when he looked at me, I knew everything was okay. The features of his face were flat, conveying not anger but thoughtfulness. Clearly, he wanted to tell me something; even if he did not know how, or did not know how much of it he should express.

His voice turned soft—a tone between library-soft and reflection. He mused, "I know I wasn't experiencing life on welfare. When you put yourself in the shoes of another, you're doing just that, putting *yourself* in their shoes."

A SNAP standpoint can never be truly known except by living it: going through it 24/7; knowing it morning, noon, and night; and by wearing the identity, and stigma, of someone on welfare. Terry evidently recognized this positional fact. Rather than claiming to have lived the experiences of a SNAP recipient, Terry understood that he had gone through the entire process as a participant in a social experiment. He was also a participant who had memories, a lifetime of received wisdom, and preconceived notions about SNAP that would not—*could not*—be true of a legitimate recipient. The accomplishment, then, lies not in becoming another but in imagining one's own life with fewer options, making the experience more real, more immediate, and more experientially honest.

"I'm a man with a lot of hobbies"—golfing, guns, and travel were mentioned in the context of favorite pastimes. "I assume if I couldn't even buy cough medicine, I wouldn't be able to do a fraction of the things that give me pleasure. That would suck."

Maybe we ought to be looking for experiences that amplify this dissonance—the contrast between an individual's sense of self and who they think they would be if their life (and monthly incomes) looked different. The challenge looks to have had this effect on Terry, increasing his empathy for SNAP recipients by helping him see that a life in poverty is no steak-and-lobster cakewalk.

That would have been the end of my story with Terry had it not been for the phone call I received the following day. Donna, his daughter—the one with misplaced priorities—Googled me and found my office number. "It's about my dad—," she stated, her voice uncertain, but then she repeated it, her voice more confident. "It's about my dad; he's fine but I wanted to share something that he didn't tell you the other day."

Turns out, while laid up with the flu, Terry cozied up with Barbara Ehrenreich's modern classic *Nickle and Dimed*, where the author chronicled her attempts to get by on minimum wage in three states. Donna gave him the book years ago. It sat unread on his bookshelf until some days prior, while at the tail end of the food stamp challenge.

Coincidence? At that time, I was not sure. Now, I think the challenge had something to do with this uncharacteristic action—it was Donna who told me her father's favorite author was Bill O'Reilly, a former Fox News host, the political antithesis of Ehrenreich.

I have been clear from the start that my argument is not that facts no longer matter. They matter, but so do a lot of other things. And without attention to the latter, we can forget about the former getting through and changing hearts and minds.

I return to this point in later chapters. Some experiments where designed to explore if heartland experiences have any influence on what makes it into one's head. But is it such a stretch to think that certain experiences might have the power to short-circuit particular deeply ingrained filters that result in motivated reasoning? I have a friend who came out to his parents a little over ten years ago. It was a conversation that played out many years in his head before escaping through his mouth. He was terrified of how they might respond, being the type of Catholics who attend mass even while on vacation. Fortunately, they did not disown him on the spot, as my friend feared they might. After exchanging tears and hugs, the very next thing his parents did was ask questions. And after that, they sought to educate themselves on the subject. Doing this, for instance, taught them that the term *sexual preference* is wildly problematic, as it implies that sexual orientation is a choice. My friend assures me that these actions would not have been imaginable had he not come out to them.

This also helps me speak to the possible criticism that I only present cases where new empathy presents itself—that I found, in other words, exactly what I went looking for. While thrilled at finding evidence that people like Terry were moved by these contrived experiences, I am just as interested in the processes leading up to these outcomes. In other words, it is as much about the journey as the destination.

Making Memories That Stick

Changes in attitudes and behaviors can be fickle. We have seen this repeatedly when financial incentives are used, for instance, with preventative care. For decades, behavioral economists have been looking at the efficacy of external rewards for motivating people to give up smoking,[19] change their diet,[20] and exercise regularly.[21] Across a wide variety of incentivized behavioral changes, once the "carrot" is taken away, behavior often returns to prereward states.[22]

Were the changes I observed among the SNAP challenge participants similarly ephemeral?

To better speak to that question, I decided to call the Marthas and Terrys of the experiment some 12 months later to request one last interview. I was especially interested in knowing whether the attitudinal changes recorded in the short-term had held.

To make this possible, I interviewed only those who reported *notable* changes to their attitudes, post-SNAP challenge. This winnowed out the number of people who could have been interviewed from 22 to 12. That all 12 enthusiastically received my invitation foreshadowed things to come.

Lisa lit up every room she entered. Her face was bright and inviting, as were her eyes. She was quick to anger and even quicker to laugh, though neither lasted very long.

Lisa lived in Denver and taught economics and business classes at one of the city's many postsecondary institutions. Her political pedigree differed a bit from Martha's and Terry's. She was a registered Independent who leaned either left or right, depending on the issue.[23] "I voted against George W. the first time, then for him, then for McCain, before becoming an Obama fan," she proudly explained, brandishing her independent streak. She cast her ballot for Gary Johnson, the Libertarian Party candidate, in the 2016 presidential election.

In our first interview, she described herself as socially and culturally liberal but fiscally conservative. She was pro–gay marriage and pro-choice but "against most entitlement programs," adding later, "people ought to be able to do what they want with and to their lives and bodies." Those freedoms also come with risks, she told me, coldly explaining that "when you fail, you need to take responsibility for it and not expect a handout."

She had also shown anger during our first interview when the subject had turned to welfare and entitlement programs more generally. That conversation was quite animated, as those subjects had come up often. I still vividly recall one instance: she grabbed two handfuls of hair and made a primal groan at the mention of government programs in Scandinavian countries. "*Please*, don't get me started on what I think about *those* countries!"

I would not be mentioning this, however, if nothing had changed. Some of Lisa's attitudes had shifted—some a lot. I was curious about where those changed perceptions stood a year later.

Lisa was comfortable reflecting on her memories of the SNAP challenge. "The smell of tuna or bad coffee. Anytime I boil water. The few times I go too long without eating and my stomach starts to rebel—you know that feeling, when your stomach is turning and tossing?"

She was responding to a question about whether the SNAP challenge ever enters her mind and, if so, how. What I found striking about her answers was how the experiences were being recalled. Her memories were physical, immediate, and intimate rather than abstract, cognitive, or factual.

She struggled to elaborate when I asked her to do so, finding it hard to put the feelings into words. At one point she said, frustration building in her eyes and across her face, "It's hard to explain. You'll just have to trust me when I say the lessons of the challenge are still with me. *Why*, I can't say."

Her attitudes about welfare and entitlement programs sounded a lot like what I had heard 12 months earlier, in the interview immediately after the challenge. The experiment had mellowed her on subjects that had, prior to the exercise, animated her actions and speech. Those 12 months had done little to diminish those changes, as she remained slow to provoke when talking about SNAP. Again, this position is 180-degrees from what I experienced during our first meeting.

To probe the matter further, I read to her from the transcript of our first interview. The specific text recited came from one of those moments where Lisa's anger had flashed. It included the line about how "people ought to be able to do what they want" while needing "to take responsibility for" whatever life throws at you.

She started to smile before I could finish, and once I had, she laughed in a slightly bashful way. "Did I really say that?" she asked, with a look on her face that clearly indicated recognition that she had. Then her smile faded.

"Look, we all need to take responsibility for our choices. But an argument could be made that programs like SNAP increase choice by putting options on the table that wouldn't otherwise be available."

I took her use of passive voice to suggest that her change of heart, while sincere, still sat uneasily with her other beliefs about government programs; she still railed against Big Government, for example. Nevertheless, the attitudes Lisa acquired through the challenge seem to have held. Her experience aligns with what I found talking with the 11 others, though, of course, each recalled the shifts differently. What all 12 individuals seemed to have shared, however, was a curious inability to talk about *why* the lesson of the SNAP challenge still stays within them.

Lyle was another who I had reached out to. He was a recently retired high-school teacher who also had very few positive things to say about welfare programs when first interviewed. When asked if he still thought about those two weeks, he mentioned how "there is something about the challenge that lingers with me; I don't even have to be doing something related to food." Then he told me that the day prior, while driving, he had remembered a cost-cutting strategy employed while taking the challenge.

"The memory of me reusing teabags rushed to mind, totally out of the blue. Maybe because a song was playing on the radio; maybe because I had this meeting today with you. It wasn't the first time something like that happened, having a memory like that about the exercise."

Embodied-memory scholars write about how certain experiences register as intense pulses of recognition, "knowledge" that struggles to be contained within the bounds of representation, within words or numbers. Cultural theorist Brian Massumi refers to these events as memory without content.[24] It might be a smell, triggering a flood of emotions and sensations and causing us to feel a long-deceased grandparent's embrace. My paternal grandmother left us in the early 1980s. I was a small child. The smell of Dove bar soap—*her* soap—still causes me to experience feelings generated back when *The A-Team* and *The Dukes of Hazzard* were entertaining eight-year-old boys like myself on a weekly basis. Or a taste, which teleports us to childhood, with the anxieties and comforts that accompany this age—in my case, my mom's Christmas fudge. We all know the power of such memories, even though we cannot fully communicate what precisely "it" is that we are remembering.

We acquire this "intelligence" not by reading or by being told things but by *doing* something. We acquire it by taking a journey, to the heartland.

CHAPTER 3

We're Being Pulled Apart

T HIS CHAPTER OFFERS a break from previous chapters to speak to some specific relationships driving our current cultural unrest. It is not exhaustive. An entire book could not cover everything threatening modern democratic societies. The following overview is just that, an overview—a pointed survey of certain factors pulling us apart. The purpose of taking this tangent is based on my hope that by understanding the scope and depth of the problem, we can acquire an appreciation for the type of solutions required—namely, ones that are bold, intentional, well-funded, coordinated, and . . . heartfelt.

Movers, Stayers, and the Anxieties of Globalization

Sitting in my car, engine off and windows down, I was enjoying a glorious fall afternoon in a park on the outskirts of Madison, Wisconsin. Craig was watching his daughters, so I fully expected him to be late, which he was by a few minutes. Then a car pulled parallel with my own.

Expecting to see a 40-something male staring back at me, I did a doubletake when two young faces came into view—young girls, maybe eight and ten, respectively. They had scooted next to each other in the back seat and were eyeing me intently. Sisters for sure, their faces were three-quarters framed by tightly curled puffs of fleecy red locks.

I could not help but smile and give an animated two-handed wave, eliciting giggling as both exchanged quick glances.

A few minutes later, Craig and I found a bench to occupy that gave us a view of the playground, set against cornfields and pasture. The view was perfectly composed, the variegated hues of green—corn and grassland foregrounded by well-manicured Kentucky bluegrass. The picture-like qualities were enhanced by the fact that the grazing cattle seemed not to move. The ten or so Angus just stood there, like an ensemble of models waiting to have their portrait painted.

Reflecting on the view, Craig announced, "I wish there was a way to freeze all this." Confused, I broke my gaze and turned, giving him my best *What?* face. He continued, elaborating on what he meant by "all this." "Rural life . . . rural lifestyles . . . rural culture. *Rural communities*," he intoned.

Craig was a two-time Obama voter who not only voted for Trump in 2016 but volunteered for his presidential campaign. I was there to hear his story, to learn why he had this presidential change of heart.

Craig lived in a small town located a short drive from where we sat. It had seen its nonwhite population increase considerably after the opening of a turkey processing plant. Rather than engender an appreciation for difference, this increase in the community's diversity had the opposite effect, at least on folks like Craig.

"Times are hard enough the way it is," he exclaimed, rapping a closed fist on the seat between us. It was not clear to me whether he was blaming this difficulty on the town's recent economic struggles or its demographic shift. My guess is that he was unable to disentangle the two.

The freshly outlined jaw muscles on his profile warned me to proceed with caution. Craig was showing signs of frustration. I thus welcomed the relief his daughters brought with their high-pitched cry, "Daddy!" From the swing, they howled in unison as the older sibling gave the other a well-executed underdog. Tension lifted. I plodded forward.

"How has the turkey plant impacted the community? The Somali immigrants—."

"Don't!" Cutting me off, Craig awkwardly picked up his sunglasses that had been sitting between us and started looking at them as if they might contain the secrets of the universe. A few seconds passed before he added, "Don't get me started about the processing plant, the immigrants, globalization, the Washington Consensus."

The Washington Consensus refers to a handful of economic policy prescriptions promoted by institutions like the World Bank and the International Monetary Fund. More generally, the term is used to describe the macroeconomic policies promoted by so-called globalists and free-trade advocates, which is the vernacular I understood Craig to be using.[1] It is not a term heard often in casual conversation, though I should have expected as much from someone who religiously reads the *Wall Street Journal*.

We returned to the subject of how his community had changed: the loss of a family-owned lumberyard; the closing of a True Value Hardware store; the shuttering of a cabinet manufacturing plant. This all came before the turkey processing plant's opening. Community leaders, in Craig's words, "had little choice but to cut a devil's bargain by handing out tax breaks to bring in those jobs, positions that would be doled out to a bunch of foreigners." He failed to add that this was only because longtime locals like Craig did not find the repetitive labor of butchering poultry to their liking.

A mix of conditional factors influence how individuals respond to local ethnic diversity. Yet there is strong evidence correlating increasing economic deprivation among individuals with their expression of more negative attitudes toward non-European ethnic groups.[2] This link is especially pronounced when coupled with an out-group moving into a traditionally homogeneous (read: white) social space, which describes Craig's community to a T.[3] While *economic* status might be beyond the control of folks like Craig, his frustration with globalization stems in part from his inability to do anything about it; community norms dictating *social* status remain within the purview of historically dominant groups. That then becomes the yardstick by which one is judged—for example, How does someone dress? Do they speak with an accent? What are their hobbies?

I have taken many friends into rural establishments. I grew up in a nonmetropolitan county in northeastern Iowa, my hometown less than a three-hour drive to Craig's front door. Some of these establishments were popular haunts with local farmers, where I would alert them to the fact that they were surrounded by millionaires. The look I would get in return was one of disbelief. "You'd never know it by looking at these people," would be a typical response. That is not to deny the presence of stratification and status in these spaces. Wealth still matters among farmers near my boyhood town; you better believe they're keeping tabs on who owns the most land and who's about to lose their dairy herd to the bank. Yet the pecking order is equally based on nonmaterial factors, like work ethic, how English is spoken, how well behaved one's kids are, and whether the household goes to church regularly.

Craig's comments were especially striking given that I had spoken to his neighbor Nick the day prior. In direct contrast to Craig's views, Nick was bullish when talking about his community's future. And much of that enthusiasm was *because of* the community's influx of Somali immigrants.

I mentioned this to Craig. His response was immediate, beginning with a furrowing of brows that were large and full. Craig used his eyes and forehead as some use their hands when talking. In Craig's case, the brow furrow was his way of conveying what might be best described as a cross between displeasure and indignation.

"Nick's a nice guy but he wasn't born there," Craig explained—
there being Craig's hometown. He turned to look at his girls before
adding, "It's different for those of us who have spent our lives there;
we've stayed and we can see how much things are changing."

There is a body of longitudinal research that talks about "movers"
(folks like Nick) and "stayers" (the Craigs of the world).[4] While increased diversity is positively correlated with decreased community
attachment among stayers, among movers the effect is less clear as it also
depends on the diversity level of the environment they moved out of.

Craig was a stayer, so his contrasting views about the community
relative to those expressed by Nick made sense. Craig's household
was also struggling financially. The vacant building on Main Street
that housed the now-shuttered True Value Hardware store was his
wife's home away from home for almost 15 years. Starting as a cashier
while in high school, she eventually rose through the ranks. When the
store closed, she was its assistant manager. Craig still works, though
the salaries of rural teachers are modest. His wife was the breadwin-
ner. Though not poor—"the cost of living here is low, fortunately," he
volunteered—he talked repeatedly about how times had been better.
Nick, in contrast, commutes 30 minutes to his practice located in
another town. He is a dentist.

Globalization, demographic transitions at the community level,
and widening economic disparities at all levels are making people
uneasy. And the trend line isn't heading in a promising direction.
We can now say, definitively, that the Tax Cuts and Jobs Act of 2017
delivered none of the "trickle down" initially promised by the Republican Congress and President Trump. Business investment in fact
slowed in 2019.[5] And then came COVID. While effectively shutting
down economies around the world during 2020, we are now seeing a
"K" recovery. This is where pockets of the economy are truly soaring
(Zoom, Amazon, Walmart, etc.), while others (airlines, restaurants

and hotels, entertainment and the arts) show no hope of recovery in the immediate term.

Speaking of COVID: what have been some of the responses out of Washington, DC, to keep the economy, and our food chains, open during this global pandemic? President Trump signed an executive order in April 2020 that declared meatpacking plants critical infrastructure. At the signing, he told reporters that the order would address "liability problems," mentioning specifically Tyson Foods.[6] The liability problems he was referring to related to worker safety. Meatpacking plants have been the source of numerous coronavirus clusters. As of September 2020, more than 200 meat plant workers in the US have died of COVID-19.[7] The executive order signaled a greater interest in the continued production of meat than the safety of workers. Based on the clear disdain expressed by Craig toward the darker-skinned immigrants working at his town's turkey processing plant, I am sure he would have supported Trump's order.

By talking about geopolitical and economic realities, I am not excusing the Craigs of the world. We can point to the grievances voiced by white, middle-class Americans without pardoning their unconscious (i.e., colorblind) or explicit biases. One way to do this is by recognizing how these grievances are *shared*—yes, the Craigs of the world are suffering, and so too are, say, those meat plant workers who were forced to work in the middle of a global pandemic. Doing this is important on many levels, one of which is to ensure that (white) victimization does not act as a Trojan Horse for white supremacy. A sense of victimization has proven a powerful organizing force, especially in the age of Twitter, where otherwise unconnected individuals can be inspired to, say, go to Wisconsin, rifle in hand, and carry out vigilante justice.[8]

But of course, knowing that economic realities matter changes nothing—at least, not until people start feeling differently about the world. No revolutions without widespread empathetic revelations.

Geographic Sorting

Arnold was 62 years old. Short black hair sat atop a head with heavy jowls and narrow eyes that made him always look as though in pain. I was given his name from a retired Iowa state senator when I asked for names of past supporters who were nonpartisan. Digging through old emails, I formulated a specific ask: "I would like names of anyone who has welcomed legislation built on working across political aisles."

Arnold lived outside of Cedar Rapids, Iowa, with his wife and two golden retrievers. He had volunteered on numerous campaigns for the aforementioned retired politician. Granted, that had been in the early 2000s. I know people can change, but geez; the Arnold I met was the polar opposite of the person who had been described to me. The senator had developed a reputation in the state for being a moderate Republican. I had therefore expected Arnold to be cut from the same nonideologue cloth.

I found Arnold sitting behind a small round table ringed by lawn chairs in his machine shed. Facing a television mounted on a wall decorated with John Deere and Chicago Bears paraphernalia, the image of the then-alive Senator McCain flashed on the screen.

"John McCain's a RINO." The ultimate insult that can be leveled at another Republican: RINO—Republican in Name Only. It is a pejorative term used to describe Republicans who are not sufficiently conservative, usually also in reference to those willing to cooperate with Democrats.

It was days after McCain had cast the decisive vote against the Republicans' final proposal to replace the Affordable Care Act, the so-called "skinny repeal" option, which failed 49–51. We were 20 minutes into the interview when a segment on the future of Obamacare appeared on *Fox and Friends,* the weekday morning news show on the Fox News Channel. The television had been muted. Yet the sight of McCain was too much for Arnold, provoking the RINO comment.

Perhaps it was naive of me not to expect this. We are—and in 2017 things were no different—living in a moment of hyperpartisan-ship. Litmus tests abound. "Real" Democrats are not allowed to like anything about Trump's policies, just as bipartisan Republicans cast in the image of McCain find themselves on the receiving end of RINO insults. Moderates like Arnold in this environment either adapt, die, or retire. The Iowa state senator who connected me with Arnold took the latter route, while Arnold opted for a different path. And most know what happened to McCain: he lost his battle to cancer about a year after my meeting with Arnold.

Arnold owned a successful cement-mixing company. "Revenues are up more than 500 percent since the Great Recession," he told me. Economic deprivation did not appear to be driving his evolution from moderate to hyperpartisan. I picked up on something else as the more likely culprit: sorting—geographic and social sorting in particular.

"I had the opportunity to sell my business and retire with my wife to Seattle. Our four grandkids live there—both daughters with their husbands," Arnold explained. By his own account, the move "would have made sense," adding that the offer made to acquire his business "was generous and would have allowed us to live comfortably within a few minutes of our babies"—his grandkids at the time all under 10.

Why, then, was Arnold still putting in 50-plus-hour workweeks?

"I couldn't bring myself to living there"—*there*, again, being Se-attle. I thought he was going to mention the climate. The rain. The lack of sun. The cool summers.

Nope. "The liberals."

I should not have been surprised. How many times have I heard left-leaning acquaintances say they would never move to deep-red states.

It is called geographic sorting: the idea that people sort them-selves into communities that are home to others like them.[9] (Social scientists observed early a tendency in social groups for similar people to be connected together—the "birds of a feather flock together" phenomenon, called *homophily*, meaning love of the same.)[10] This likewanting-to-be-with-like can refer to political affiliation—Arnold's desire to live next to other conservatives places him in this category. More often, however, partisans end up self-sorting because of their tastes for residence characteristics, which are in turn correlated with their political affiliations.[11] Democrats, for instance, tend to prefer walkable neighborhoods, community diversity, and places that celebrate that difference, in part because many of them do not hold to white, heteronormative identities. Republicans, in contrast, prefer communities with less residential density, have opportunities for worship, and have organizations and institutions (e.g., schools, VFWs, gun clubs) that celebrate more conservative values. Arnold exhibited some of these traits, too.

For instance, he expressed displeasure over the thought of selling his "gator"—a four-wheel-drive utility vehicle that looks like an overbuilt golf cart. He used the vehicle to inspect his property's fence line, a "need" that would disappear had he moved to Seattle. He also derived great enjoyment from target shooting on his property. "The thought of having to join a range, and *paying* range fees and *driving* to it. Not ideal," he lamented.

Is this sorting the *result* of rising political tribalism or the *cause* of it? The data are not sufficiently clear to answer this question. If anything, evidence points to both factors as being at work.[12]

What is clear is that we are interacting increasingly with others who look, think, and vote as we do. We see this in activities like online dating, where possible suitors' political identities are being factored in as much as their educational levels.[13] Internet use is especially tied to one's political beliefs. To quote one study: "media consumers favor certain websites not only due to their content but also due to their audience"—meaning we visit certain web addresses because we know others who think and look like us do, too.[14] Homophily also sorts us into the shops we patronize and the organizations we belong to.[15] And through these "birds of a feather" interactions, biases are amplified.

Arnold admitted to "not knowing a single Clinton or Sanders supporter"—Hillary and Bernie, respectively. It was embellishment, as I recall him saying earlier that his two daughters were registered Democrats. Yet his point was well taken: Arnold's social networks consist largely of others who share his view of the world. This is no better illustrated than by his sister's ouster from his life in the wake of the 2016 presidential election. "She's the worst kind of liberal," Arnold explained when describing sister Shirly. He then added with emphasis, "*She votes.*"

"What's the saying? If you can't say anything nice to the person, you don't say anything at all. It's easier to send cards during the holidays and at birthdays. We'd just argue otherwise," he nonchalantly explained. I know a lot of others who think exactly like Arnold, and I bet you do, too. We know that network homophily—like-only-hanging-around-with-like: i.e., Arnold's social network—facilitates motivated reasoning and amplifies the effects of selective media exposure.[16] So: you will probably agree with me when I say, there's nothing you can tell them to make them think otherwise about those not of their ingroup. And that's my point.

But not everyone I know is like Arnold. Some are more motivated than others to have their beliefs, especially political ones, challenged. One variable that appears to matter, in terms of shaping level of commitment to a given outlook, is exposure to heterogeneous messages and networks, which supports what I am trying to accomplish here. Can expanding one's social network really alter how motivated someone is to be a tribal, close-minded partisan? Looks like it.

The National Election Study (ANES), started in 1948, provides the oldest continuous series of survey data investigating electoral behavior and attitudes in the US. Using this data, a team of researchers attempted to determine how social network diversity impacts voters' political views.[17] Of particular value were data from the question, "From time to time, people discuss government, elections and politics with other people. I'd like to ask you about the people with whom you discuss these matters. These people might or might not be relatives. Can you think of anyone?"

As expected, the data supported the thesis about how motivated reasoning thrives in informationally closed networks—so-called echo chambers, where essentially the same stuff is parroted. Yet there is also a more hopeful story to tell, about how citizens who interacted with supporters from both Left and Right more freely provided reasons for liking and disliking presidential candidates from both major political parties. In other words, to quote from the study, "citizens exposed to heterogeneous messages are less likely to hold a polarized attitude toward a candidate," which is to say, "they are more likely to develop an attitude toward the candidate that incorporates positive and negative assessments."[18]

The Marketization of Everyday Life

Googling "money makes you a jerk" will yield over 6 million hits. Titles from the first couple of web pages tell you plenty about the articles' content: "How having money makes you a jerk"; "If you were rich, you'd be a jerk too"; "Science closes in on the reason rich people are jerks"; "Why being rich makes you a jerk"; "It's not your imagination—rich people are jerks, say science"; and "Does money make you mean?" The articles reference a wealth of research that has been published, most since the early 2000s, on how money changes us, sometimes profoundly.[19]

The thesis has been supported through dozens of novel natural and experimental observations. Participants in one study were primed by the presence of a large pile of Monopoly money. Those exposed to the play currency were less willing to help someone who "accidentally" spilled a box of pencils.[20] In another design, participants filled out questionnaires while seated in front of a computer monitor. Some had screensavers that depicted bills; others had images of fish swimming. Exposure to the former was more likely to reduce participants' willingness to work in a team and increased their likelihood of viewing themselves as having less in common with other participants.[21] In another design, subjects unscramble phrases that included words such as *salary* while a control group worked with nonmonetary terms. The group that worked with nonmonetary words spent an average of three minutes on a difficult puzzle before reaching out for help, while members of the money group resisted reaching out to others for assistance for more than five minutes. Moreover, those who unscrambled nonmonetary phrases spent, on average, twice as much time assisting peers as did those who had been primed with the money cues.

Numerous natural observations have also been made that lend further support to the idea that money changes us. Researchers in one study observed a busy four-way intersection and recorded that luxury-car drivers were more likely to cut off other motorists instead of waiting to turn. The behavior was the same for both men and women upper-class drivers, regardless of the time of day or the amount of traffic.[22] Another paper reports that drivers of luxury vehicles were more likely to speed up to pass a pedestrian that was trying to use a crosswalk rather than waiting for the pedestrian to pass, even after making eye contact with the individual.[23]

These studies regularly correlate wealth with individualistic values if not outright selfish behavior; the last study mentioned is titled "How Wealth Reduces Compassion." While an eye-grabbing title, it overstates matters. More likely, the fault lies less in wealth and money per se than in how these phenomena are being put to work.

Markets slash transaction costs for certain activities. What I mean is that you do not have to be friendly or even have trust in people you engage with in markets thanks to regulations and contract law. Heck, you don't even need to speak the same language in the market-place. Have you used Uber? This celebrated example of the "sharing" economy requires absolutely no personal interaction between driver and rider. *None whatsoever.*

Yet this has come with its own costs. Thanks to their increasing ubiquity, marketized exchanges are starting to catch up with us in deleterious ways. This is not just my opinion. Several prominent economists are beginning to ponder the limits of markets, not because we cannot place a price on everything but because of what happens when we do.[24]

The earliest studies to explore this phenomenon in a systematic way date to the 1980s. Psychologists Gerald Marwell and Ruth Ames gave students tokens, which could be placed into either a hypothetical individual investment (a private good) or a collective investment (a public good).[25] For every token invested in the private good, each participant received a small amount of money. Each token invested in the public good was awarded a larger amount of money. These awards were then pooled and equally shared among all participants, including those who had not invested in the public good. Economic theory explains why people should not want to voluntarily contribute to a public good. Nobody wants to contribute if it helps people who do not, the "free riders." Running through numerous samples of students, Marwell and Ames found consistency in the fact that roughly 49 percent were willing to place their tokens into the collective investment. Curiously, the economists in the group proved a consistent outlier. They averaged investing only 24 percent of their tokens in the public good. This research has since been replicated.[26] The titles of these studies range from the bland, such as "Does studying economics inhibit cooperation?" to the downright scandalous, as in "Do economists make bad citizens?" and "(Why) do selfish people self-select in economics?"[27]

There are thousands of examples of how markets leave their mark on social norms, resulting in, to use economist-speak, the crowding out of nonmarket (e.g., prosocial, we-focused) motivations.[28] One frequently cited example of this comes from Israel and involved a childcare center that struggled with getting parents to pick their children up on time.[29] Adults were arriving late, which required that the center pay staff to stay after hours. To resolve the issue, the center imposed a fine for tardy pickups.

Expecting this solution to work, the administrators were surprised to discover that it had the opposite effect. Parents' lateness *increased*. What happened?

The fine changed the norm. Parents who previously felt guilt and who mostly tried to arrive on time started to view the fine as a fee. As a fee, the extra childcare began to be understood as a service that parents were entitled to if they chose to pay.

There are countless ways that marketization, by way of monetizing a once nonmonetized action, can lead to the erosion of prosocial attitudes and behaviors. I have seen this in my own research.[30]

MachineryLink Sharing is a Kansas City company that had been leasing combines before attempting something new. Billing itself as a sharing platform—it's "Uber, but for tractors," to quote one article about the platform[31]—the firm promises to deliver a win-win. The farmers leasing—let's be honest: *sharing* this isn't—idle equipment can earn a little extra money, while farmers who cannot afford, or who choose not, to buy these machines outright have access to the newest models at a fraction of their retail cost.

"Welcome to tractor alley!" Bart exclaimed with outstretched arms as I stepped out of my rental car. I was in north-central Kansas, planting my feet on the front yard of a three-thousand-plus acre farm. Bart, a 40-something corn, soybean, and sorghum farmer, was about to show me his collection of "John Deere toys." He was not the first farmer to describe equipment to me in these terms, though in this case the description struck me as too casual given the scale of the investments involved. "More than 2 million," Bart replied after I asked how much the equipment cost.

I mention this to put the cost of using MachineryLink Sharing into perspective. "Generally, you'll spend anywhere between $20,000 and $50,000 to use my equipment," Bart told me. He showed me an invoice that backed up this claim. It was for a tractor he had leased for 200 hours at a cost of $38,000 to someone in Washington State. While a lot of money, it is a fraction of what it would cost to purchase the same piece of equipment outright.

It is not so much this "sharing" platform that interests me here but in how its introduction into Bart's life changed how he related to friends. To tell this story, I need to start at the end, with my parting conversation with Bart. The visit ended as it began, among those "toys."

I was in the cab of his new four-track John Deere tractor—aptly named: it has four tracks, each in the shape of a triangle, instead of wheels. The height afforded me a clear view of the horizon. I saw another vehicle's dust rising in the distance. After it passed, Bart informed me that the man driving was Scott, a neighbor. "He's not a huge fan of this piece of equipment," he added. I thought perhaps Scott was a Case IH or Massey Ferguson fan—some farmers take their tractor brand affiliations to the extreme. Nope; turns out it was not that Scott disliked this particular tractor as much as this particular tractor's owner.

Scott and Bart had known each other since childhood. And their parents, too—lifelong neighbors. The two families have been living side by side since the 1950s and have been borrowing each other's equipment the entire time. That ended, however, when Bart started using that sharing platform. With Bart now trucking his pieces of equipment across the country, they were no longer available to be borrowed. He even admitted that his involvement with Machinery-Link "hasn't exactly been a plus as far as neighborly relations are concerned."

When explaining how this rift with his lifelong neighbor came about, he admitted that the platform caused him to view his relationship with Scott differently. What had been a nonmarket relationship has since become commodified.

As Bart put it, "I can make $20,000 or $30,000, or I can let my neighbor use it for free. You do the math. Unless I start charging the guy a comparable rate, the tractor's going to the guy who's going to pay."

What does any of this have to do with today's hyperpartisanship? Conviviality has taken a hit as social interactions become increasingly viewed as commensurate with market exchanges—in Bart's case, what was once about social norms is now about making a buck. I do not believe money per se is responsible for the jerkification of society. What is problematic are the ways we organize our everyday activities around it.

As those practices proliferate, the need for empathy as a moderating force intensifies.

Media, Market Fragmentation, and Outrage

It would have been easy to start this chapter talking about the proliferation of politicized talk radio and cable programming. I didn't because I fear we sometimes give these talking heads too much credit for the state of things. Again, no one thing is at fault. But it would be naive of me to not mention what others have called the rise of outrage—a form of political communication that glosses over the complexity of issues and focuses instead on melodrama, mockery, and impending doom.[32]

The growth of this industry is undeniable. Take the case of radio: the number of all-talk stations tripled in a span of roughly the last 15 years. Radio personalities like the late-Rush Limbaugh and Sean Hannity together reached almost 30 million people daily, which is not including those who might tune into Hannity's eponymous nightly television program. To put that number into some perspective, some 30 million children participate in USDA's National School Lunch Program daily.[33]

In the days before cable and satellite radio, in an era when the Big Three—ABC, CBS, and NBC—dominated the airwaves, the first commandment among station executives was, *Thou shalt not offend*. The most successful shows were those with the least objectionable content as the aim was to entertain the broadest segment of people while offending the fewest. Ever notice how vanilla programming was back then?

The expansion of choice turned this business model on its head. As audiences became fragmented, advertisers' expectations changed. Today, cable networks and radio stations are increasingly aimed at smaller, more like-minded audiences. As Berry and Sobieraj write in their book *The Outrage Industry*, partisan personalities "are not succeeding *despite* offending some segments of the audience but *because* they do so."[34]

Outlandish personalities, of all political persuasions, offer advertisers something very important, namely, a direct line into the homes, cars, minds, and souls of key demographics. If a personality is peddling fear on their show, for example, and you are in the home security business, what better way to reach your target audience! Two of Sean Hannity's leading sponsors are, not coincidently, ADT and SimpliSafe home security systems.[35] Home and personal security companies can now speak directly to potential users for a fraction of the cost of an advert placed during *NBC Nightly News*, which has an overall larger audience but roughly the same number of eyeballs from those key demographics.

From a policy standpoint, there are things we can do to combat all this hate and divisiveness emanating from various media platforms, like breaking up media monopolies. In 1983, 90 percent of what we saw, heard, and read was controlled by 50 companies. Fast-forward to 2020. Six corporations—Comcast, News Corp, Disney, Viacom, Time Warner, and CBS—now control that 90 percent.[36] Even that "local" media station that has been with your family for generations, there is a good chance it is part of a monopoly—like that beer in your refrigerator posing as "craft"; better check to see if it's owned by Anheuser-Busch InBev. Sinclair Broadcast Group owns or operates 294 television stations across the US in 89 markets, ranging in size from a couple of million to a couple of thousand. In 2018, the sports blog Deadspin famously published a video that spliced together footage of dozens of Sinclair anchors from around the country at these "local" stations reading from the same pro-Trump script.[37] When Bernie Sanders claims that America is "owned and controlled by a small number of multi-billionaires," he is also talking about media ownership.[38] And he is right.[39]

Another option is the regulation of hate speech, though I know that when you try to regulate speech, you risk unintentionally pushing it to places that are beyond the reach of governments and policing bodies. Once there, those spewing hate become emboldened. They also become connected to others who feel exactly the same way. Remember that stuff written earlier about the dangers of homogeneous networks: they're bad from the standpoint of their impacts on members' close-mindedness.

We are seeing this happen with the rise of the so-called dark web, which refers to areas of the internet that cannot be accessed with a normal web browser.[40] The suspect in the 2019 massacre that left 51 Muslims dead in Christchurch, New Zealand, posted his infamous manifesto online—a hate-filled train wreck unworthy of the code it is written with. It did not take long for law enforcement to scrub the web clean of its existence, with ongoing monitoring to this day to ensure it never sees the light of day. Nevertheless, the document lives in the web's darkest corners for all like-minded zealots to draw inspiration from,[41] where it is untouchable by law enforcement agencies thanks to totally decentralized hosting.[42]

There will be sightings in the following chapters of the outrage industry, mainly as I set the scene—a radio program airing in the background or images on a television that momentarily get pulled into the foreground of the conversation. During my travels, social media was more than the occasional sighting. For some respondents, these platforms helped turn them into who they were, namely, motivated reasoners who saw the world in highly partisan, black-and-white terms.

I have gotten to know a number of self-described conservatives, for instance, who are leaving Facebook and YouTube because of what they see as policies that limit their freedoms—especially that of free speech and those relating to the Second Amendment. YouTube has drawn their ire in particular because of the platform's recent move to demonetize videos with gun content. Demonetization is the process wherein independent content creators are denied paid advertisements in their video, thus reducing, if not outright eliminating (if there are no sponsors), their ability to generate income from the video-hosting site.

Nat sticks out prominently in my mind in this respect, in part because he was a prominent YouTube personality in some circles but mostly because he was *deep* in the rabbit role. I met with Nat in Arizona, where he was actively involved in making Mohave County, which covers the northwest corner of Arizona, the first local jurisdiction in the state to declare itself a "Second Amendment Sanctuary County"—a movement declaring that local law enforcement officials will ignore federal laws seen as infringing on gun rights. We were discussing how he used the internet to promote his politics.

At one point, while discussing how he learned that his own channel had become demonetized, he said, "Creators producing conservative content, whether it's about guns, shooting, fake news attacking Trump, the Sandy Hook Hoax"—yeah, he was one of *those* guys—"are losing their voice on the platform as YouTube is being pressured by the Left to shutdown conservative channels."

While Nat's comments are telling about the ideological leanings and cognitive filters that give those outlooks legitimacy, what he did as a result of these perceived insults is why I mention him here. Like hundreds of thousands of other like-minded individuals, Nat found new social media ecosystems to inhabit, with names like BitChute, DTube, and QubeTV. These platforms are not on the so-called dark web. Anyone with a browser can access this content. They represent a reorganization of the internet that parallels what happened earlier, first to radio programming and later to television—the specialization of content that produces echo chambers where the same messages become transmitted and, eventually, normalized.

A 2020 study by the Pew Research Center found that YouTube users outnumber those of any other platform in the US, with 73 percent of US adults identifying as users. Facebook, at 69 percent, comes in a close second. No other platform is used by more than 40 percent of US adults.[43] Given this concentration of users, it is easy at this moment to say, "Regulate and restrict speech!" But in doing this, we are hastening the decentralization of use and pushing people into their respective tribal corners, spaces where preaching to the choir isn't just the norm but the expectation.

"I know the lamestream media is fake, with those polls saying Trump and his policies lack support of most Americans," Nat said, adding, "I don't know anyone not 100 percent behind President Trump. How can you expect me to trust conventional news outlets when what they're saying goes entirely against what I'm hearing?" This is what happens when motivated reasoning is left to thrive and when people find social media (and social network) ecosystems to inhabit where they hear exactly what they expect, and want, to hear. We can focus on the means by which hate and outrage are communicated, or we can try to address the reasons why hate has the audience it does. Even if we could abolish this speech, we would not abolish hate. And steps to accomplish the former always risk exacerbating incivility. As Nat's story reminds us, no one likes to be told what they can and cannot say. That is not how you create a revolution, at least not one premised on empathy.

CHAPTER 4

Farming Familiarity

H IS FACE IS STRIKING in its contrasts: skin, pale and thin, crisscrossed with bluish veins; hair, black and thick; eyes, fierce and deeply set. I was visiting with Nick. A large, bulk of a man, he had lived in Colorado since 2008. It was late summer, 2017. We were sitting adjacent one another, each on a large log resting cut-side up, in the yard behind his 100-plus-year-old American Foursquare. It was early enough in the day that the sun's rays were filtered through the leaves of the neighbor's maple trees. The blowing wind cast about the scent of someone's fresh-cut grass.

He spoke slowly, as I had imagined a rural Mainer would—the majority of my exposure to the dialect comes from reading Stephen King novels.

"Ayuh, he's no choirboy," Nick says, "with sweethahts from here to Californier." We were talking about President Trump. "He taps something deep in a lot of people, his views on *immigration* and *Muslims*, so supporters overlook those other parts."

Nick, a lifelong registered Republican, lamented how the 2016 election was the first time he submitted a presidential ballot without voting for a candidate. "I couldn't bring myself to vote for the guy. Maybe ten years ago I could have. Not ta-day."

He was by no means the only longtime Republican who found Trump's 2016 campaign difficult to support, and many other Republicans abandoned Trump in the 2020 election. But that is not why I am talking about Nick here. I am more interested in the confession that he could imagine being a supporter in his past.

To tell this story, however, I have to first go back to 2011. That was the year I embarked on a unique study.[1]

I have been asking social science–type questions about food systems since my time as a graduate student at Iowa State University in the late 1990s: Who wins/loses as a result of these networks? How does food create community? How is it divisive? One question that has been hanging over the literature since I started paying attention to it centers on the social consequences of alternative food networks; I'm talking about things like farmers' markets and Community Supported Agriculture (CSA) platforms. Truth is, it is challenging to say what those consequences are, in part because of the nature of most social science research designs. Research conducted on the subject typically looks at one snapshot in time, after people have become enmeshed within the activity.[2] This is not meant as a critique of my critical food studies friends. The list of expenses associated with longitudinal qualitative research tends to be long and tenure clocks short.

What we are left with, then, are data that do not distinguish between behaviors and attitudes gained from participation and those that drew them to the practices in the first place. Maybe picking carrots with immigrants made you more empathetic to people different from yourself. Or did you decide to participate in this experience because you *already harbored* caring sentiments toward others outside of your immediate political tribe? The classic chicken-and-egg question in social science research: did the behavior elicit the attitude change or did preexisting attitudes animate the behavior? To answer that question, a researcher needs to, first, identify people before exposure and, then, follow them over time.

While most people have been separated from food production for a long time, we have seen in recent decades a proliferation of social spaces meant to reconnect us. Interestingly, these gatherings span conventional political and ideological divides. Some of my most partisan acquaintances get food from these places, which means they hold exciting potential for engendering something even bigger than a food revolution. Of course, not all should be expected to do this. I am reminded of a farmers' market in Atlanta that was located in a gated community—empathy and checkpoints don't mix. Then, there was the CSA in California that only dropped off at sites not serviced by public transportation, effectively limiting membership to those who owned, or could borrow, a car.

The longitudinal research reported here began when I identified new members of CSA businesses along a 175-mile stretch that ran from the Colorado communities of Fort Collins to Pueblo, anchored in the center by Denver. Nick was among those included in this sample. CSAs consist of eaters coming together and pledging support to a farm operation so that growers and consumers mutually support and share the risks and benefits of food production. Surveys place the number of CSAs in the US at between 7,500 and 13,000.[3] CSAs typically offer at least one of the following two options: drop-off and/or volunteer. The drop-off model refers to a membership where the CSA delivers food to a prearranged drop-off site. Consumers may never set foot on the farm and may have limited interactions with those growing their food. A volunteer model, conversely, refers to an arrangement allowing eaters to work off some of their membership by means of planting, weeding, harvesting, and so forth. The individuals mentioned below enrolled in the volunteer model.

Once identified, individuals were interviewed and asked a range of questions about who they bought food from and why, their views toward different social groups, and their community-oriented behaviors. The goal: establish a baseline.

It is easy to dismiss CSAs as serving a niche market.[4] Though they account for between $200 to $300 million in direct-to-consumer sales, that total represents less than 7 percent of the $3+ billion in direct-to-consumer sales by farms.[5] A wellspring of new jobs and capital investments these platforms are not. This makes it easy to view these networks skeptically, at least when considered narrowly through an economic lens.[6] This stance is as unfortunate as it is unfair. We are shortchanging ourselves by limiting framings of value to, say, *jobs* lost and gained, tax *dollars* collected, and *pounds* of produce sold. The experiences these platforms afford could be more important than 100 new jobs, for the reasons below.

Setting the Stage

The day was late. The sun, already behind the mountains, was detectable only by the crimson streaks shooting off the peaked horizon. I was sitting on the porch of Nick's house. Side by side, on large, white wicker chairs, we looked west toward the fading light, while Nick explained his decision to join the local CSA.

"A friend told me about it. Told me the food tastes better, healthier too. Not sure about it being healthier. But God's truth, those tomatoes they gave me, awful tasty."

Generally, eaters pay in advance for their share, which will cover the anticipated costs of the farm operation and farmer's salary. This arrangement means that the growers and consumers are both invested in the agricultural process, and the risk is shared rather than individualized. Fruit and vegetable farmers servicing urban markets usually eat all their losses when faced with poor harvests resulting from unfavorable weather or pests—there is no federally subsidized crop insurance for these growers. In CSAs, farmers and consumers benefit when times are good, just as they feel the pinch together when times are not. Farmers also benefit under this arrangement by not having to worry as much about marketing, as food is spoken for before seeds touch Earth.

Nick's CSA gave shareholders the option to work off part of their annual subscription. This involved, in Nick's case, spending a few hours a week doing whatever the season demanded, usually something having to do with planting, weeding, and harvesting. He did this because he wanted to. He mentioned his parents having a garden when he was younger. It was an experience he recalled favorably. "It could have been Christly hot but I didn't care; I enjoyed it." Not that he needed to work off a portion of the fee. The proud owner of a chain of successful furniture stores, Nick's privilege stood in contrast to many others who "volunteered" because they had to. This made for an interesting natural experiment.

The state of Colorado is roughly 87 percent white, compared to the national average of ~76 percent.[7] Many of its metropolitan areas, unlike the bastions of diversity in other states,[8] look as white as the average Academy Award nominee, though some counties, as we will soon see, are experiencing rapid demographic shifts. In Fort Collins, where I live, the US Census Bureau places those identifying as "white" at just south of 90 percent.[9] I was therefore struck walking onto the farm for the first time, encountering whites, blacks, and Latinos in roughly equal numbers working side by side.

Coming within earshot of the gardens, I was assaulted with a loud, ringing, staccato laugh, such as one hears on the stage. "Yessah!" A large man wearing a blue polo shirt, khaki shorts, and a Boston Red Sox baseball cap nodded approvingly at a young, darker-skinned man facing him in an adjacent row. I later learned that this 22-year-old had been born and raised in the southern Mexican state of Chiapas. The man with the unmistakable laugh, who stood a full head taller, has already been introduced. Hearing Nick's laugh is one of the first memories I have of this particular CSA.

After he returned to picking beans, my eyes settled on the nearest movement. Ten yards ahead, an older African American woman—a retired college professor, I learned—was cutting flowers and handing them to a white, first-generation college student in her late teens. Their silent efficiency suggested a history together, a synchronized, wordless rhythm that comes only with practice. Neither looked at the other, focusing instead on the task at hand, though both wore those gentle smiles we carry around when content without fully realizing it.

I started this longitudinal experiment back in 2011. Since then, I have been interviewing, observing, and participating alongside the same participants every year. For some participants, those data go back to 2011. In other cases, as new members joined the CSA, those relations are newer. Yet the goal remains the same for all: to discern whether those CSA experiences had any influence on what the participants thought and did.

The rationale for joining a CSA with the volunteer option was never expressed to me by anyone as about getting to know people from different political tribes. Wanting to meet people might have been mentioned on occasion. "I suppose it would be nice to meet different people," as Cindy explained. But what they really wanted was to meet *new* people who were *like* them. Cindy's rejoinder captures this point. "I really want to meet some other moms"—she had a one-year-old and a fulltime nanny—"someone I might be able to go have coffee with during the day." Never mind that not all mothers have time to go for coffee in the middle of the day. What she really meant is that she wanted to meet other upper-middle-class mothers like herself. Cindy was an attorney, her husband a surgeon.

One common motivator mentioned for joining the CSA lay in the belief that the foods tasted better and that they were healthier—Nick was quoted earlier making exactly this point. Research looking into why people participate in these spaces shows there is more to animating this behavior than people seeking out tasty, healthy food. And while the price of these foods matters, demand is more inelastic when compared to goods from more conventional supply chains, which is economist-speak for saying people continue to purchase these foods even after a price hike.[10] Food scholars have also described participation in these alternative food networks as being about identity maintenance, which itself might be in response to societal expectations—for example, being a "good mother."[11] There is also evidence indicating that some go looking for status in these spaces as much as food.[12]

Could these asocial motivations open a door to experiences that engender empathy?

Rebecca's Transformation

The sun shone bright as I approached the building. The wind, though bringing welcome relief in the midday heat, made its presence continually known, like a persistent child, foreshadowing what lurked in the dark clouds to the west. I was on the eastern plains of Colorado, about a 45-minute drive from Denver. The property was owned by a couple whom I had been introduced to a few weeks prior at a pancake breakfast in a nearby rural community to raise money for their volunteer firefighter department.

It was 2016, and I was on the lookout for Rebecca. Bryan, her husband, brought me to the machine shed—their "office." They co-owned a diesel mechanic business.

I heard her first, a sharp metal-on-metal clank, a socket wrench dropping, followed by cussing. She walked out from behind the tractor holding her thumb, but only long enough to grab a socket extender.

"Belt broke," Bryan explained. His tone was matter-of-fact, suggesting that this repair was routine.

Climbing up into the cab, Rebecca started the beast. A high-pitched squeal of the starter followed by the roar of ignition. She jumped off and moved close to where she had been working. Eyes closed, head tilted downward, leaning against a wrench that was as long as her leg. She listened to her handiwork. This tableau offered an unforgettable sense of scale, accentuated by her indifference to the belts buzzing and the chest-pounding rumble filling the enclosed space. It reminded me of the children's tale of the mouse that pulled a thorn from an elephant's foot, if the elephant were green and spewed diesel exhaust out its nose.

The original plan had been to conduct the interview there, in the shed. Instead, we found ourselves dashing for the house amid thunderclaps that heralded the storm's arrival.

The rain came shortly thereafter, sounding like a murder of crows scurrying on the tin roof. We were sitting around the kitchen table. The clatter had gotten so loud at one point that it drowned out the *tic-tic-tic* of the metal kettle heating up on the stovetop. As Bryan sat to my right, Rebecca, already settled directly across from me, spoke in tones reflecting a mix of frustration and embarrassment.

"They're fresh off the boat, I swear. I'm not sure if I should work with them or report 'em."

She was dipping her steeping tea bag in and out of the hot liquid, her head inches above the cup. The steam rose into her face before being dispersed by fluttering eyelashes.

"Don't get me wrong; I'm not saying illegals are bad people. But we've got laws for a reason."

Rebecca and Bryan had recently joined a CSA. For years they'd had their own garden. This year they had opted for something different. They had lost most of their crop to hail the previous two growing seasons. Joining a CSA seemed like a sensible compromise given the climatological realities of the state. Bryan explained: "As you know, we can go months over the summer without a drop of rain, so we had to irrigate like crazy." With summer highs regularly between 90 and 100+

degrees Fahrenheit and humidity well below 50 percent, irrigation is key. "All that money spent on irrigation and all the work on our part, then throw in the occasional summer hail storm," Bryan said, "and you'll see why we decided to go the CSA route." They settled on a CSA roughly 20 miles away, one that allows members to work in exchange for a reduced rate. Their attraction to the arrangement centered mostly on the fact that both enjoyed gardening. "While a poor substitute for having your own garden, it's better than nothing," was how Bryan put it. They also had a seven-year-old daughter. Both singled out the importance of teaching her about where food comes from, while making sure she appreciates the value of a good day's work.

Rebecca's comments about having "laws for a reason" had been her response to my question about potential challenges associated with their CSA membership. It had less to do with the perceived legal status of the CSA's brown-skinned members and more to do with where these members came from. "I'm sure they're citizens, really," Rebecca assured me. The sense I got was that she applied the "illegals" label liberally to any brown-skinned individual who spoke broken English with what colloquially is called a Spanish accent.

Having followed these two for three years, I'd learned that the "illegals" reference was a method of deflection. Much like a magician uses movement and flair to mask what is really going on, Rebecca and Bryan relied on stereotypes to hide their, shall we say, *discomfort*. This tends to happen when someone is forced to engage for the first time with those who have been Othered by one's own political tribe.

That discomfort was there in Rebecca's remark about how a neighboring town's new postmaster speaks Spanish, a development due to the community's changing demographic. It was also there in Bryan's awkward laugh as he joked about the taco food trucks that were parking near the CSA gardens. These remarks and responses shared a root system. Racist attitudes? Perhaps. But, of course, Rebecca and Bryan wouldn't have identified as "racists." Not that I asked. Having known people who comfortably use the n-word while claiming to disavow racism, I don't see that question (i.e., "Are you a racist?") as providing much of a litmus test. How these people reconcile *that*, in case you're wondering, falls back on claims of being colorblind. Something like, *I direct derogatory terms at everyone, including in reference to myself!* To paraphrase Chimamanda Ngozi Adichie, a Nigerian writer, the Rebeccas and Bryans of the world are unable to see their own actions and words as racist because race doesn't really exist for them because it has never been a barrier, whereas people of color don't have that choice.[13]

High school sweethearts, Rebecca and Bryan were both born and raised in Colorado. They spent most of their lives in a rural county that has experienced considerable demographic change. From more than 87 percent white in 1980, the county has diversified. Fewer than 60 percent of its roughly 30,000 residents are white, with the county's growing Latino population making up 35 percent. I could make excuses, without excusing their behavior—something about how these two had not spent much of their lives around people with brown skin. But I know a lot of people who grew up in a nearly all-white environment who would never express the sentiments that these two did. These two are also Obama-Democrats-turned-Trump-supporters. I cannot call them Trump Republicans because they have been registered Democrats during the time I've known them. Though they eventually moved to an adjoining county closer to Denver, they still talked about their town as if they were "stayers"—they now live less than 15 minutes from Rebecca's parents. Recall my prior description of stayers: long-term members of a community undergoing demographic change and economic hardship.[14] Stayers are more likely to express negative attitudes toward increasing diversity, often blaming local economic hardship on those new to the community who do not look like the average stayer.

Bryan explained, "It isn't that we have anything against immigrants." Telling me this, his eyes grew wide as his hands came up and palms turned toward me. It was a defensive posture that I've seen before, as if in response to a claim that he harbored xenophobic attitudes. He then added, "What we have a problem with are foreigners coming in and taking jobs when longtime members of the community are unemployed because there isn't enough work to go around."

Not long after, Bryan reminded me that they voted twice for Obama. This came after being asked about Trump's rhetoric toward immigrants.[15] Rebecca and Bryan harbored clear resentments toward Latinos. Their struggle, regardless of how well they actually negotiated matters, involved trying to find ways to give those antipathies release in a way that would not betray their other sensibilities, namely, knowing it is not all right to be a racist and bigot.

That was our first interview, followed later that year with visits to their CSA. We have had a few other interviews after that, the last in late 2019. None, however, were as surprising as the interview that followed the first, which happened almost two years later. I would have reinterviewed them sooner, but life got in the way: a family death had postponed my second home visit.

The air was cool outside, even for a mid-May day at roughly 5,000-feet elevation. Large east- and west-facing picture windows caused the indoor temperature to rise quickly, perhaps too quickly, as I soon regretted not having a t-shirt beneath my sweatshirt. I was back at Rebecca's and Bryan's house, waiting for Rebecca to return to the room.

She had disappeared shortly after greeting me at the front door. A couple of minutes passed, and I began to wonder, *Did I come at a bad time?* Just as I was about to vocalize my misgivings, she returned in possession of a framed picture and an ear-to-ear smile. I also heard Bryan enter through the back mudroom—the "snap" of the tightly sprung screen door as effective as any bell.

She approached, holding the photo in front of her, picture-side turned up. I recognized their yard immediately. The machine shed could be seen in the background. Its doors, large, open. The effect created a memorable contrast—bright, midday Colorado sunshine surrounding a big, black hole created by the building's shadowed inside.

The faces in the photo's center eluded my recollection. Other than Rebecca and Bryan, whom I recognized, I could not identify the others.

"Recognize anyone?" Rebecca asked. "Anyone other than Bryan and me?"

The faces were shadowed by hats. As the picture had been taken midday, noses, eyes, and mouths were cast in darkness. Each figure was given a closer look as I tried to mentally reconstruct the face based on the visible features. Names came to mind. *Iliana. Eduardo. Antonio.*

"Those are people from the CSA," I exclaimed, with a mix of relief and excitement.

The picture was taken a year prior. One of Rebecca's and Bryan's neighbors owns and operates a corn maze. Rebecca and Bryan invited "friends"—their word—over to their house the previous fall, with the enticement of Rebecca's chili and free entry to their neighbor's maze. The picture was taken at some point between these events.

These were the same two individuals who had expressed anxiety toward Latinos, if not toward these very people, just two years prior. Since then, they had willfully expanded their circle of friends to include members from the very group that they once disparaged. It was a pretty remarkable shift.

What they told me during that second interview was *not* what I was expecting, especially when it came to their positions toward darker-skinned immigrants. Have you ever gone away from a place for an extended period and on return sensed a change within the first few minutes, in its tempo, vibe, and overall tenor? If so, you can relate to what I intuited in that interview with Rebecca and Bryan.

No one variable explains why Rebecca and Bryan underwent the changes they did. Whatever happened, though, is largely attributable to the experiences afforded them by their CSA, practices that helped them learn to replace caricatures with peopled familiarities.

"Did I really say *that*?" Rebecca asked. I had just read from the transcript of our initial interview—the part that included the quote, "They're fresh off the boat, I swear. I'm not sure if I should work with them or report 'em." Red-faced, she confessed to having been embarrassed, though she did not exactly take the words back. "I was a different person back then" is how she explained the comments.

A lot of respondents used those very words to defend prior comments and to situate where they were standing in relation to the past. *I was a different person.* It was as if the CSA experiences fundamentally changed who they were.[16] I had seen this in others, too; with a couple of years of these experiences under their belts, the selves I later interviewed had developed their capacity for empathy.

I was grateful to have transcripts of earlier interviews, as they served like time capsules—most social scientists do not have the benefit of time travel. People have terrible memory recall abilities.[17] We can rarely remember what we ate last week. If we are unable to recall intimate acts of putting something into our bodies, forget about expecting people to know how they felt about an issue or group of people years in the past. Participants could not believe some of the things they had said when first interviewed. *All* were embarrassed by something. It might have been a comment, a term, or a suggestion. One person, for instance, was shocked he had said that all Mexicans were lazy. This embarrassment might have been expressed by words, as in, *I am embarrassed I said* . . . For others, the tell was blushing, usually coupled with a good bit of stammering;

they seemed sufficiently shaken that they could not initially form a complete sentence.

I was also grateful for having been present to watch some of these encounters. If people cannot accurately recall past feelings, they certainly cannot be expected to describe the experiences that afforded those changes.

I remember one, the summer prior to that second interview. We were picking sweet corn. Rebecca was a few stalks away in the same row from me, so I could see and hear everything that transpired. She was showing a young Costa Rican mother—she must have been in her early or mid-20s—how to know when to pick an ear of corn without disturbing the husk. Rebecca's instructions were not getting through; she tended to talk fast when frustrated, and someone for whom English was a second or perhaps a third language would likely be frustrated as well. Annoyance spilling over, Rebecca straightened up. She looked in my direction, closed her eyes.

The pause had a calming effect, for when she opened her eyes she looked composed and ready to hand out another lesson. This time, Rebecca slowly reached for the young women's hand. The student nodded slightly before having her skin touched, assenting to the breech of her personal space.

"Here—feel this?" Rebecca asked, touching a big fat ear, "Good; it's good!" Reaching for another ear, "Now this. This isn't ready."

The young pupil asserted that the lesson was getting through. "Ah, *Sí.* Yes, *Sí*!"

They were effectively holding hands and smiling while looking straight into each other's eyes. It was a sweet moment to watch, no doubt, and could easily have been written off as just that—a *moment.* Connect the dots, however, and you might arrive at a different conclusion.

When Nick Met Juliette

It was summer of 2016, and I was back at Nick's CSA. A lot of us had gathered to help cage tomatoes. The event had a festive air as parents involved their children in the activity. Having helped cage in previous years, I knew it to be a good time to catch up with people. Neither is the work particularly hard, nor does it require the same level of concentration as, say, cutting asparagus or tying up cabbage heads. This particular CSA prided itself in growing various varieties of tomatoes, including many in the lauded "heirloom" category.

Her button nose and high and sharp cheekbones, each side ornamented by a dimple when she smiled, were framed by a mass of wavy hair so dark it looked blue. The small, lively woman—Juliette—bounced as she walked, creating the unforgettable effect where half her face went in and out of blackness when viewed from the front as her hair swung in cadence with every step. She greeted me with a handshake and Nick with a hug.

I found the friendship curious. Nick was right of center with his politics. He self-identified as a conservative and was a registered Republican; my notes from 2011 contained other tidbits of information about his political leanings. I had spied a copy of *American Rifleman* and a large Liberty gun safe in his family room, suggesting that he was a Second Amendment guy. I also had seen a copy of Pat Buchanan's 2001 book *The Death of the West* on a bookshelf in the kitchen.

Juliette, in contrast, was a self-professing progressive liberal. She had been born and raised in Denver, and her biography differed considerably from Nick's. About 15 years his junior, Juliette had two children (he was childless) and worked for a house-cleaning service. She was also bisexual. Even their preferred local transportation *modus operandi* were worlds apart—his 5 Series BMW to her Schwinn seven-speed, supplemented with Denver's light rail system. Yet here they were, hugging it out like age-old friends.

Both confessed to having learned something from the other. *Learned*: their word. As they explained what transpired, Juliette professed to "coming around on guns," and Nick was "rethinking his positions on gay rights and immigration." They were learning to *empathize*. The word comes from the Greek *empatheia*—*em* (into) and *pathos* (feeling): to penetrate as much as to perceive.

After about five hours of work interspersed between a lot of talking and laughing, the tomato cages were positioned and anchored. The effect added considerable height to a garden that at sunrise looked flat, save for where the sweet corn was growing. Sitting on a picnic table, having a late lunch, Nick and I talked about his relationship with Juliette, as well as other relationships fostered in this space. He was reflecting on the friendships made over the last few years because of the CSA, particularly those that might have surprised the "old Nick." (He referred to "pre-CSA Nick" in the third person, which in itself is telling.) Juliette was mentioned, as were a couple of others. "Immigrants from Mexico" was how he described most of them, even though some of them came from other Spanish-speaking countries.

Nick was trying to put into words why Juliette's sexual orientation was not an issue for him anymore, "though it might have been," he admitted, "back in the day."

I asked him to explain what prompted this shift.

"Hard tellin'. There wasn't any one thing. It's not like we talked about why she likes women." I took this comment to mean that the facts of the case were never discussed. After adjusting his bottom on the seat, he continued.

"I got to know her first, not Juliette the lesbian but Juliette. Juliette, the person."

To his credit, Nick did not shrink from the challenge of trying to explain why he made the friends he did. He asked, speaking more to himself than to me, "How did I come around to seeing people instead of parodies?" *Parodies*: he volunteered the term, essentially confessing that his "old" view of some groups was based on exaggerated falsehoods.

Before answering his own question, Nick stared off into the distance. A bead of sweat had dropped from his nose, breaking the trance. His answer consisted of rattling off examples of things he had done with Juliette, activities ranging from sharing recipes to making raised garden beds and picking green beans. I was struck by all the verbs. It was not passive learning that elicited these changes but something else.

Included was the time Juliette shared with Nick a recipe for salad dressing made with Red Savina habañero—a hotter cultivar derived from the better-known habañero pepper. Nick continued to use the recipe even though he thought it gave him diarrhea.

Laughing, he explained his bowels' response as, "the Muthah of all—let's say it wouldn't stop and leave it there."

"We still laugh about it to this day," he continued. "It's an intimate thing to share between people, if you can wrap your mind around that idea."

This eventually led to more regular exchanges between the two, of recipes and then later of food, which started when Nick gifted Juliette some of his homemade clam chowder.

To empathize with another requires some extension into them, to sense the world through their eyes, with their mouth, or by their pain. We can do this by query. *What do you eat? What do you do? Who do you love?* Communication alone, however, only scratches the surface when it comes to fostering care. Think of love. What could anyone ever simply *say* to make you fall in love with them? In all this talk about talk, there are physical elements that get missed. These activities—remember all those verbs used by Nick—go beyond asking and verbally responding and can include eating what another eats, learning to build raised beds with another, even laughing over "giving" a newfound friend an upset stomach.

For those wanting to know what exactly turned "pre-CSA Nick" into who he is today, you will have to forgive my silence. We need to rebel against the trappings of methodological individualism—the idea that the world *can* be reduced to discrete variables. We're seeing a revolution taking place across the academy based on such a rebellion. Contemporary efforts in the cognitive sciences, for instance, have responded to this conceptual messiness by talking about "4E cognition," which represents a holistic understanding of the mind as embodied, embedded, enacted, and extended—an update of the integrated and visceral description of knowing advocated some 80 years ago by phenomenologist Maurice Merleau-Ponty.[18]

My inability, then, to tell you exactly what made Nick change is not a limitation that can be remedied with more research or better data. It is, rather, an honest representation of what ultimately isn't entirely representable. As with any good story, the power to explain and describe rests less in its discrimination of detail and more in its unity, or gestalt.

Practicing Values

Values are understood as providing a foundation for seeing the world.[19] We know, for instance, that one's foundational moral frames—about care, authority, fairness, and loyalty[20]—are better at predicting political attitudes than political ideology and partisanship.[21] Those most successful in bridging tribal divides around hot-button topics like climate change select frames that better speak to the values of their intended audience.[22]

Talk to people using language that they'll respond to. That is certainly easy enough to do. All of today's thorny issues—for example, inequality, immigration, health care reform, racial justice, food insecurity—require collaboration, compromise, and cross-cultural understanding. But does it really change anything? If we ultimately cannot stand being in the same room with each other, what have we solved? There's difference of opinion. Then there's difference based on some not recognizing the humanity of others, which is what really concerns me.

I met Nicole on my second trip to the garden, right after she ran into the farm's toolshed door. A short, energetic thirtysomething, she was apparently so accustomed to marching right in that she did not notice the padlocked latch until it was too late.

It was her first year with the CSA, and she had already started making friends. One of them, Josh, was not far away when she had her accident. She had been locating a hoe for him. Evidently, they had been talking about Obamacare when the conversation took a pause long enough for Nicole to retrieve the tool.

Hoes in hand, the two weeded, and I joined. That was how I knew they were talking about the Patient Protection and Affordable Care Act before Nicole's accident.

"The government already has its nose in too many things. I don't need it managing my health care on top of everything else. Do you want the government telling you what treatments you can and can't have? And vaccines: *forced* vaccinations?"

Josh was not having any of it. "That's too conspiratorial. Be reasonable."

That was how it went for the next few minutes: a conversation directed *at* rather than *with* the other.

I mention this exchange because it exemplifies others I had with Nicole early on, which helped me identify one of her moral frames. She was an *individualist*. As a foundational value, individualism has been defined by those who study moral frames as manifesting "attitudes toward social orderings that expect individuals to secure their own well-being without assistance or interference from society."[23] A statement used to evaluate whether one holds and exhibits this value is, "The government interferes far too much in our everyday lives."[24] Nicole's prior quote leaves little doubt about how she would have answered this question during her first year with the CSA.

Nicole's boundless energy made her a popular figure at the farm. Quick to make friends and slow to lose them, she was still a member when I reached out to schedule the fourth interview, in 2017.

Each interview after that first year had elements that surprised me. Whether something Nicole said or did, I saw evidence that her attitudes, beliefs, and maybe even values were undergoing a change. Perhaps the most notable change concerned how closely she held to the ideology of individualism.

Nicole's two dearest friends from the CSA, Kim and Christa, were SNAP recipients, the program I described earlier that offers nutrition assistance to eligible, low-income individuals and families. Eligibility requires a gross monthly income that is generally at or below 130 percent of the poverty line, which, in my state of Colorado, translates to an annual income cap of about $16,000 for a one-person household.

"These are the first friends I've ever had who qualify for government assistance," she told me. At first, Nicole did not talk about money with Kim and Christa. That is not something people generally discuss, even among friends. Nevertheless, Nicole suspected early on that the other two "had a more difficult go of it" than she. Nicole, an accountant, described her position as "solidly middle class."

An entire year passed before they got around to talking about why they each opted to work at the farm in exchange for a lower membership rate. That proved a watershed moment.

"We stopped projecting the person we thought we needed to be and started being ourselves, if that makes sense," Kim said at one point, when we were all together.

It did make sense, though I am grateful for the elaboration that followed. The three proceeded to share life stories. They told me about divorce, temporary homelessness, transportation challenges, illnesses, and food insecurity. Later that day, after Kim and Christa left for work, Nicole shared with me about how deeply those stories had impacted her.

"Reading about poverty or seeing it in a movie can't compare to knowing someone who's living it—seeing the exhaustion in their eyes, hearing it in their voice."

This brings me back to the observation about Nicole's evolving projection of individualistic values, a stance that cannot be divorced from where she ended up on subjects relating to welfare and poverty-related government programs. Through the practices afforded by the CSA, Nicole experienced how working together—in a word, *collaboration*—helped to make certain things possible for individuals lacking financial resources. She shared tools and equipment and was party to exchanges where the "currency" was social capital—where members, for example, relied on each other for childcare or bartered labor and skills to get toilets installed, salsa made, and lawns aerated. Nicole's CSA-based relationships eventually spilled over beyond the farm, resulting in, for instance, her preparing others' tax returns in exchange for new brake pads on her car and a lawn mower repair. Perhaps these "lessons" were palatable to Nicole because of how they were packaged: as community.

The individualism/collectivism *dichotomy* is too stark. It implies those in the former camp prioritize individual freedoms, while suggesting the latter do not have it in them to be selfish. I know plenty of card-carrying Libertarians and Republicans who would score "high individualist" on a moral frame survey who wouldn't hesitate to sacrifice for kin and peers. And some have already sacrificed for Country. A lost limb. A missed birth of a child. PTSD. The moral to glean from this observation, then, is that even so-called individualists welcome engaging with sentiments that speak to the value of "us" rather than "I." The trick, however, is making sure that the expanded *us* doesn't come at the expense of a scapegoated *them*.

In one of those later interviews, the subject returned to the role of government. I had expected to hear from the Nicole who had debated Obamacare with Josh six years prior. This was someone who once told me that "welfare incentivizes laziness." At the time, she was driving a Ford Ranger that had the bumper sticker "Socialized Medicine: Nanny State Health Care at Cadillac Policy Prices."

What Nicole said surprised me. There was no mention of the Nanny State or Big Government in that final interview, though the opportunities to drop the terms were plenty. She still talked about the importance of things like individual liberty and responsibility. But it was interspersed with what sounded like . . . progovernment sentiments.

With the sun low in the sky we stood leaning against the closed tailgate of her Toyota Tundra. I was halfway through the questions on my interview guide when she confessed being distracted. She was distraught about her girlfriends, Kim and Christa.

Kim recently lost her aunt, who doubled as a babysitter. Christa, meanwhile, had to pick up a second job. "They're both facing the cold reality of maybe not being able to do this anymore." With the word *this*, Nicole's right hand went out, palm up, in the direction of the farm.

Her face held a faraway look. Though looking in my direction, she wasn't looking *at* me. A few seconds lapsed before she spoke, gravely, as if the haze that had disappeared from her eyes settled in her throat.

"It's not fair for them, you know, having to do it all on their own. I've seen it here—you too, I'm sure. Sometimes the surest route to individual freedom is through others, friends, organizations. Hell, even the government can play a role if it's done right."

I am pretty good at holding a poker face throughout these conversations. You never want to upend an interview with a look that causes a respondent to filter their answers or, worse, cut the interview short. Maybe it was exhaustion. It had been a long day. I felt the look of surprise on my face at the same moment I saw it register on hers. Fortunately, Nicole took it in stride.

"Sometimes support comes from within the community and sometimes not. I'm not talking about making people dependent." She gave some examples, noted earlier, of how people were empowered in that space by sharing—of tools, labor, and skills.

"It's about creating additional individual freedoms through *interdependence*," she intoned.

It is hard to overstate how out of character such a statement would have been had it come from Nicole on our first meeting. This was the same person, after all, who tried to connect Obamacare to forced vaccinations. This Nicole held a deep suspicion of anything that resulted in one person needing another, to say nothing of her prior unwillingness to reconcile the tension between wanting to privilege her individual liberties even if that meant cutting into yours. That's the challenge with interdependence, to see ourselves reflected in every other human while also respecting and honoring difference.

It might have been out of character for that Nicole. But this wasn't that, especially if we accept the growing consensus in the academy about what it means to be human, as embodied, embedded, enacted, and extended. Following that, this Nicole inhabited the world in myriad ways that distinguished her from whom I first met after she had run into that toolshed door. The most accurate thing to say, then, would be not that her *attitudes* changed. *She* did.

→ CHAPTER 5 ←

Working to Respect Those Who Fed Us

WE AGREED TO MEET at Stan's Tavern. Not only was it close to Venus's house, but her 73-year-old mother was the establishment's cook. The Wednesday lunch special was taco casserole, which Venus assured me was delicious.

Arriving first, I approached the counter and let a bearded barman pour me a suspect coffee before I selected a booth against the large picture window near the front. Staring at the liquid's surface, I was trying to determine just how badly I needed a caffeinated pick-me-up when she approached.

"I wouldn't drink that if I were you," she said before pushing her sunglasses up, catching her hair in a complicated bundle of brown curls.

Before I could say anything, she made her move to sit. She did not drop in one fell swoop, as I had. Venus's moves were more choreographed. Both hands flat on the table. A pivot of the hips. The shuffling of feet. The ordeal ended with a protracted groan, lowering herself slowly into place as legs, hips, and arms coordinated a soft landing.

The look on my face, a mix of concern and confusion, elicited from Venus an immediate explanation. "Sore—back, butt, legs. Hurts to sit. Don't drink water unless I have to," adding after a short pause, "hurts to squat."

This was my doing. I did not intend for anyone to hurt from what we had done, though I did warn Venus and others at the beginning that it was a distinct possibility. She was in good spirits, taking the pain in stride. Putting her immobility in perspective, she reflected on her situation.

"Yeah, I'm sore, but it was a good experience. Had fun, learned a couple things. Having a sore butt for a day or two is a small price to pay. It's not like I have to do it for a living, thank the Lord."

Venus had participated in an all-day berry boot camp. Someone gave the event that name during morning instructions. By noon, it had assumed a place in the group's common lexicon.

I was sitting in that bar in rural California talking with a devoted Trump supporter. In a prior interview, she talked of backing a "closed border immigration policy," though when she was pressed, her ire was mostly directed at our brown-skinned, Spanish-speaking neighbors to the south. "Canadians are fine," she told me when asked what an appropriate government response would look like if there were ever a caravan making its way south from Vancouver.

That, at least, was her stance when we spoke last—about two weeks prior, when she could still squat comfortably.

Similar to the strawberry study discussed earlier, this chapter discusses the results of two related studies to see if those earlier findings could be replicated: the first, the berry boot camp; the other, an exercise where participants detasseled corn. Were the results of the strawberry study a fluke? Let's see.

Fielding Different Perspectives

I saw the bouncy castle's steeples a half mile away. Pulling into the parking lot, I noted other sights. There was a petting zoo, face-painting stand, straw bale structures, pig race track, picnic tables, kettle corn trailer, and, beyond, the crops: berries (straw- and rasp-), a pumpkin and squash patch, and field corn for the fall maize maze. The place made farming fun, by design. As this U-pick facility explained in one of its pamphlets: "Teaching the next generation about where our food comes from for over 50 years."

I appreciate the importance of these spaces, if for no other reason than to educate eaters that strawberries do not grow on trees, and about those fruits that do. And what better way to draw people in than to make the whole experience fun?

The giddy screams could be heard coming from the large cellulose structure—a straw bale parkour course. I had walked off the parking lot's gravel before almost colliding with five early grade schoolers. They emerged from between two walls of straw, apparently pretending to be in a Minecraft world—the tallest of the group was wearing an Ender Dragon mask. As I said: F-U-N.

Yet for many, especially those making minimum wage or for whom ICE is an acronym, *fun* is not the first adjective used to describe agriculture. According to the American Farm Bureau Association, US agriculture needs between 1.5 and 2 million hired workers. Given that labor costs account for 48 percent of the production costs for fruits, and 35 percent for fresh vegetables, you would be right to believe a premium is placed on cheap labor.[1] And the cheaper—and more undocumented—in many cases, the better.[2]

As the bouncy castle came into view, I passed a strawberry field sprinkled with what were later confirmed to be immigrant laborers. The juxtaposition that day was startling: to the left, brown bent bodies wearing flannel and heavy workboots; to the right, a bouncy castle that fed the carnival-like atmosphere populated by mostly white people in shorts and short-sleeved shirts. The contrast provided a fitting reminder that distance between groups cannot only be measured in inches or feet. Those immigrant laborers could be seen from the U-pick. They were that close. Yet they might as well have been on the other side of the world. They were that invisible.

Is there a way to make more visible the bodies that populate our food system, practices with the potential to instill empathy within eaters toward those who feed us? Fast-forward approximately two weeks, when the U-pick was rented in the hope of answering that question.

The task of assembling participants for a day of backbreaking work under the hot California sun was less daunting than I thought it would be. I leaned on contacts in the area—friends of friends and in some cases friends of friends of friends. The aim was to enlist individuals who were, as I had described them then, "pro-wall and anti-immigration, the more so the better." Thirty-one individuals were recruited for the study.[3]

I rented out the strawberry portion of the U-pick for the morning, taking over the farm's raspberry beds in the afternoon. Participants were told to come covered up: long pants and sleeves, something for the head, and, if they had them, work boots. The chemical residues on the fruit at conventional strawberry and raspberry farms are excessive. One study reported a single sample of strawberries showing 20 pesticides, while more than 98 percent of the berries tested registered positive for at least one pesticide residue.[4] While keeping these chemicals out, the attire can mimic the feeling of being in a sauna, especially as the temperature in the raspberry high tunnels surpass 100 degrees Fahrenheit. On especially humid days, these enclosed spaces can make it feel like you are breathing through a damp towel, which is hard enough to do when not being physically taxed by exertion and heat.[5] I also learned that raspberries are not the only things that respond positively to high tunnels. Insects do as well. Screens might keep some pests out, but they offer little protection when it comes to aphids and mites, a reality some farmers use to justify their insecticide use. The thought of working in a tunnel populated with plants laced with pesticides gave the experience a whole new feeling—the farm we worked on was organic, but one could easily imagine otherwise. *It would be like being inside a tented house immediately after having been bug bombed,* I remember thinking.

Not only were they asked to dress like someone who did this for a living; everyone was instructed on how laborers pick to maximize their productivity. Strawberries, from what I have been told by those in the industry, require a particular technique: legs slightly spread, bent at the waste like a runner frozen mid-floor-touch. This frees both hands for the pick. I was not able to discern an industry-wide style for picking raspberries, so participants were given more leeway for that fruit, as long as they worked fast. Realizing that water breaks are a luxury for immigrant laborers, participants were also discouraged from spending too much time at the water cooler.[6]

Those gathered were instructed to use their mobile devices to capture images of their time picking. I was especially interested in seeing if and how the photos changed during the course of the day—to see, in other words, if the experience's physicality would imprint itself into the images, just as it had years earlier in the strawberry study.

The photos yielded interesting data. The day started with the group channeling their inner Ansel Adams. Countless landscape images were generated in those first hours, plus a number of selfies. A few individuals displayed some talent, creating the type of awe-inspiring and somewhat tiresome photos you would expect to find on a postcard. You know the type: where beauty is eulogized without giving personal insight. Yet by afternoon, exertion became the muse and sweat stains and dirt took over as the center of interest.

Participants were interviewed twice, roughly one week before and one week after the experience: the first to establish an attitudinal baseline, the second to see if that baseline had moved. Additional data were collected by asking participants to complete a brief survey, once before and once again after the exercise. Drawing inspiration

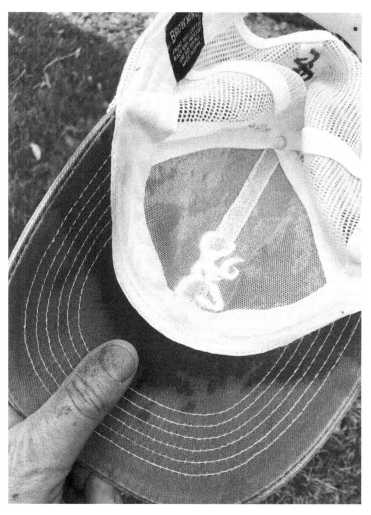

FIGURE 5.1   An example of photos taken in the afternoon.

from a survey designed to measure attitudes toward immigration by researchers at the University of Leuven, Belgium, participants were asked the following five questions, at both the front- and back-end of the experiment:[7]

How important should it be when deciding if someone ought to be able to come and live in the US that they . . .

1. Have good educational qualifications: 0 (extremely unimportant) to 10 (extremely important).

2. Speak fluent English: 0 (extremely unimportant) to 10 (extremely important).

3. Are White: 0 (extremely unimportant) to 10 (extremely important).

Furthermore . . .

4. Would you say that it is generally good or bad for the US economy that people come to live here from other countries: 0 (extremely good) to 10 (extremely bad)?

5. Would you say that people coming in through the US-Mexico border generally *fill* jobs that no one else is willing to do or *take* jobs away from Americans: 0 (fill jobs) to 10 (take jobs)?

Figure 5.2 depicts the average score for all five questions at both points in time, before and after fieldwork. My initial directive was to only enroll pro-wall and anti-immigration participants. Mission accomplished. The figure also makes clear that this group was not dead set against immigration *per se*. They had few qualms with immigrants

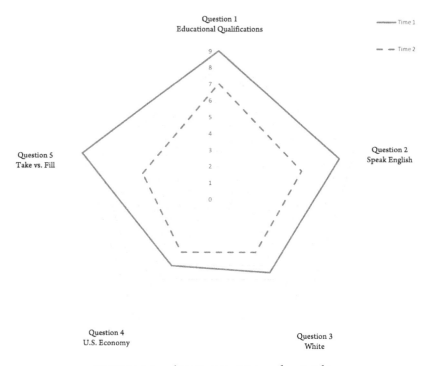

FIGURE 5.2   Average scores pre- and postpicking.

who were privileged, English-speaking, and white. Also clear from the figure is the fact that these attitudes can change.

I tried something new for this experiment, triangulating web analytics with the other data. Specifically, a temporary website was created and populated with information about industrial berry production, with particular attention placed on labor practices. The site was populated with secondary data gleaned from governmental and nongovernmental agencies.[8] An email was sent to all participants immediately after receiving their intent to participate. In addition to containing information about what lay ahead, the message directed them to that website. "For those wanting background information on industrial strawberry and raspberry production, please give this website a look," they were instructed. A few days before our second interview, participants were sent another email and reminded about the provisional hyperlink.

Behind the scenes, I monitored traffic onto the site and tracked navigation through it. As it could only be accessed with the provided link, I could be confident that those visiting had been invited to do so. When participants were interviewed, I confirmed that the link had not been shared.

Two of the 31 participants clicked on the link when it was first sent, with only one navigating past the homepage. When emailed the link for the second time, after their time in the field, 20 participants clicked through—a 900 percent increase. All navigated past the homepage.

My disappointment in the headland model of behavioral and attitudinal change, especially when it comes to overcoming hate, fear, and ignorance, is well-founded. Yet I never said information has no role to play in our politics. Facts remain a powerful force for changing hearts and minds, as long as those hearts and minds have already been primed for change. Engagements that get people to open up, to accept exposure to data that might challenge and upset established beliefs, are what we ought to be creating. Did the experience of picking berries make people *want*—it was their choice to click and subsequently navigate, after all—to learn about industrial berry production?

The answer to that question appears to be an unqualified "yes," based on the data described above. But not only that, the information on the website appears to have eventually pierced participants' cognitive filters. I know this because some parroted facts listed on the website during our second interview—for example, names of top-producing US states and counties, pesticides recently banned by the European Union, and rates of pesticide poisonings among laborers. It turns out that we can change people's minds, with the help of a little nudge from their bodies.

This nudge can take different forms; again, no one pathway can explain a change of heart. One possibility yet to be discussed involves what is known as metacognition, which simply refers to how we think about our thinking.[9] One must have confidence in one's thoughts if they are to be acted on. Motivated reasoning, coupled with selective perception, helps bolster this confidence. This reminds us that an activity does not have to change, say, an attitude or belief to engender change. Inserting doubt into one's beliefs might be sufficient. Maybe the experience of picking berries hadn't changed minds, but rather, it changed how participants thought about what they thought. By the time, then, they were confronted with that hyperlink the second time, those once strongly held prejudices had lost some of their punch. With confidence in certain beliefs waning, participants became more open to particular alternative facts. And those, then, became, eventually, the truth.

Venus's Change of Heart

The "Stan" of Stan's Tavern turned out to be the owner's bulldog. Now deceased, his photo adorned a prominent place near the bar's cash register. "He loved that damn dog," Venus explained, nodding her head in the direction of the bearded barkeep who poured me that awful coffee. We had just ordered two taco casseroles. Facing a stretch of uninterrupted time before our food was served, which turned out to be a whole two minutes, I commenced with the interview.

The process kicked off with what I thought was a safe question, something to put Venus at ease. "First impressions: what first comes to mind as you reflect on your experience picking berries?"

She watched me intently, with unblinking eyes. Having learned that that faraway look reflected contemplation, I waited patiently for her answer.

"There is no 'first comes to mind,'" she eventually volunteered, adding, "I've been thinking about that day since being out there picking."

Venus ended her answer with a shrug, a punctuation of the comment as much as an apology for not answering the question posed. There was a short pause as she thought about how to respond. Settling on a path forward, she intoned, "My *most lasting* impression would have to be how difficult the day was. It kicked my butt. I learned a lot."

From there, she launched into a lengthy monologue about how the whole experience felt. Her tempo slowly picked up, causing sentences to blend together. Bits from this monologue included: "I was so hot . . ."; ". . . my tongue was dry . . ."; ". . . I was tired . . ."; ". . . too sore to put my socks on the next day . . ."

I was especially struck by how Venus categorized these experiences. Note that she prefaced the above account as what she "learned" that day. I realize for dancers, musicians, and artists, this is an everyday occurrence. Yet I still found it refreshing to have her talk about physical feelings when providing examples of learning.

These were not the cold, hard facts celebrated by positivists but the fleshy empirics of lived experience. I took her admission to be saying that pain played an important role in helping her filter and organize knowledge.

Venus made it known near the end of our conversation, while talking about immigrants, that "the fear of them taking our jobs is misplaced." At the beginning of the experiment, negative attitudes toward nonnative laborers seemed perfectly reasonable to Venus. That was because she screened, organized, and prioritized related information through a filter of fear and anxiety. She never mentioned being scared or afraid of darker-skinned immigrants during our first interview, not in so many words. She did, however, talk about them "pilfering jobs," "taking government handouts," and "overcrowding our schools"—always in a tone laced with undercurrents of dread and fretfulness.

The tinge of fear in her tone no longer detectable, she continued: "I'll carry that day with me, long after the soreness disappears. That feeling, out there—hot, discomfort, thirst, soreness. If they're willing to do that work to make a living, God bless 'em. They're not taking that job from anyone, and I gotta respect them for that."

What I didn't hear was talk about how we need *them* to feed *us*—a common refrain among those who might be able to see a bit of themselves in others but only insofar as the latter serve as a type of sacrificial lamb in the fulfillment of "our" demands. This was especially surprising given that the group, when first interviewed, was quick to demonize and scapegoat the very population with which they later seemed to empathize. Perhaps this change had something to do with the task itself. Participants were being asked to work, an activity that holds considerable moral importance throughout much of the world. For example, a "good citizen" in modern democracies typically refers to someone with attributes associated with being a law-abiding member of society who participates in labor markets (i.e., hardworking) and economic circulations, such as by being a consumer and taxpayer. Good citizens, then, according to this formulation, are not merely recognized by the state. Perhaps even more important, good citizens have to be active in particular ways in order to fulfill this identity and positionality.[10]

This injects a lot of other questions, which I cannot fully answer, and thus complicates the picture I am trying to paint. (But I have never said the picture isn't complicated, so inject I must.) By attempting to put themselves in the shoes of an immigrant laborer, who is to say that the empathy engendered isn't a projection of their own white, middle-class, heteronormative expectations of what it means to be a (good) citizen of the US? It is not exactly a stretch to go from seeing someone as a hard worker and rule follower to then expecting them to also abide by unwritten rules pertaining to how they ought to look, talk, and dress.

It is something to think about, at least, and all the more reason to be *cautiously* optimistic when evaluating these findings.

Tall, Hot, and Xenophobic

I first met Ralph, a giant of a man, at a café less than a 20-minute drive from what he would later describe on more than one occasion as "the U-pick from hell," though always with a smirk and a glint in his eyes. He arrived early to this meeting spot, with his two tween children. When I showed up, they were playing checkers. He was supervising— all six feet, ten inches of him—occasionally offering advice. A surly looking fella in green fatigues, he cut an imposing figure. Leaving the kids to their game, we retreated to a private room that I had reserved.

It was 2018, and the immigration issue was all over the news and social media. Ralph seemed eager to talk about border security. "It's a crisis; we can't stop them coming over. Those that are here are taking welfare, and jobs. We need to look after our own first."

The "them" and "those" he was referring to are immigrants, though he never fully clarified if he was referring to only the undocumented ones. Not that an immigrant's legal status likely mattered to him; he seemed most concerned about where individuals emigrate from. His constant denigration of "Sssspanics" did little to hide his contempt for those coming into the country from our southern border.

"Sssspanics are overrunning the borders. Keep 'em out, all of 'em. We don't need them," he told me at one point.

That interview with Ralph was uncomfortable, one of the most uncomfortable of my career. The first time he used a derogatory term to describe Mexicans I asked him, politely but firmly, to choose his words more carefully in the future when in my presence. I did not wish to hear more of that rhetoric or risk having the nearby kids hear it—at least, not on my watch. His feelings were abundantly clear with that one remark; additional use would not have added any further insight.

That intervention did not stop him from expressing his distain toward this group, though he did do a better job minding his Ps and Qs from that point. The experience admittedly heightened my interest in Ralph during the day of the pick, mostly out of a sense of caution. The day started with me laying out some ground rules, like being respectful of others and only using language appropriate around elementary school children. I did not want Ralph, or anyone, hijacking the day by saying or doing something inappropriate.

Don't get me wrong; I was glad to have Ralph there with us. If these experiments can't touch the Ralphs of the world, then what's the point?

Ralph showed up early, looking the part. He wore a long-sleeved flannel shirt, gray Carhartt pants, and a bandanna wrapped around his head. Not long after arriving, he made friends with a gentleman over coffee and pastries. They both had spent an extended period in Germany and used the occasion to reminisce. Ralph's new friend was there when the country was still two, East and West. This meant that Ralph, the other man's junior by more than 10 years, did most of the listening that morning.

All that banter did nothing to slow Ralph's strawberry-picking pace. He easily outperformed the others—close to double the average of the group. When complimented on his strawberry-picking skills, he remarked absently, "Nothing to it." While he did not say it, he was clearly proud of his picking prowess. Over lunch, he used the accomplishment to remind me of his disdain toward immigrants.

"If someone my size can handle this, I'd think it would be a walk in the park for some little Ssspanics half my size."

Then came the afternoon . . .

The day was warm. The weather app on my phone read 92 degrees. I did not know the exact temperature under those raspberry tunnels, though the sweat dripping off my nose gave me an idea of what it could have been.

We were about an hour into the afternoon pick when I heard Ralph call out, "Permission to take my shirt off, boss?" He was looking at me. I had watched enough movies depicting prison labor to get the reference. Not that he was suggesting that this was a prison and I the guard. He said it in a friendly enough manner. I also know that hierarchical individualists—those who value stratification and who expect individuals to secure their own well-being—generally expect situations to be governed by someone in a position of authority.[11] Ralph, a white, male, registered Republican, checked all the right boxes. I know enough about hierarchical individualists to know one when I hear one. His comments about people needing to "pull themselves up by their bootstraps" and about how "the poor are poor for a reason" held all the hallmarks of someone harboring that particular value set.[12] This made me, in Ralph's eyes, that person of authority. Being another white male with a track record of putting him in his place no doubt had something to do with this. After I had affirmed his request with a nod, he took off his shirt. He then turned, revealing a large Celtic cross on his back—a symbol I know to be used in some white nationalist circles.[13]

It was clear that the heat and exertion was making Ralph uncomfortable. The shirt started off blue yet by early afternoon had turned violet, almost black, from perspiration. Any comfort gained by going shirtless proved short-lived. Fewer than five minutes had passed since granting his request before he blurted out, "Fuck! Damn it!"

A body the size of Ralph's is hard to navigate in the confines of a raspberry tunnel with a 10-foot ceiling. I doubt the thorns alone were behind the vulgar outburst—the first of the afternoon but not the day's last. Yet they received the majority of the Ralph's ire.

"Fucking prickly pricks! How's a guy supposed to move in here? This is ridiculous!"

Intervening, I suggested he take a break. He refused.

"I'm fine," he replied, sounding more like he was trying to convince himself than anyone, adding while pointing at the raspberry bush, "These little bastards aren't getting the better of me."

We reunited some seven days later, at the same café we had met at three weeks prior. I was eager to revisit what had happened that afternoon among the raspberries. He had someone that afternoon take a picture of him with arms stretched high. His fingertips were nearly touching the top of the tunnel, giving the appearance of a space much smaller than it actually was. I used the image as an entryway into talking about that afternoon.

Showing him that photo, I asked, "What does this picture bring to mind for you?"

Open questions like this can work on multiple levels. First, they force individuals to interpret what I am asking; the question they choose to answer can thus be as interesting as the answer they give. And second: I genuinely wanted to know his answer.

Ralph lifted his head and lowered his eyelids until they were almost closed. The lower and upper eye lashes were touching, giving the effect of filtering out what was unimportant to his answer. What was left was enough to animate a voice that had up until that point been subdued.

"We were working in a tunnel, *a tunnel*. I'm not claustrophobic, but I don't think I'd like doing that every day, not in those conditions."

A follow-up question sought clarification on that last point about what he meant by *not in those conditions*.

"A hot, humid, prickly, breezeless environment: *those* conditions," he softly crooned as if not wanting others in the restaurant to hear his answer.

When asked during the first interview if he looked at the website created for the experiment, he glibly answered through a chuckle, "Yeah, no. Didn't have time." He did look, however, prior to our second meeting at the café. This itself is not an earth-shattering behavioral change, if you can even describe it in those terms—I usually think of a behavioral change as resulting in a new habit. It is not the act, the "click," that interests me but that he voluntarily recited information from the website during that second interview.

"Almost all the strawberries produced in the US come from California, with Florida in a distant second place."

He was also able to enumerate pesticide poisoning rates: "Almost 200,000 people die every year from self-poisoning. *Self-poisoning*: I assume that's a nice way of saying 'suicide.'" That, too, came from the website. The World Health Organization places the figure at 170,000 annually.[14]

He had not just visited the website; he had studied it. Noting this observation, I asked why.

He looked almost—embarrassed? Hesitant, maybe? I cannot quite explain what I saw on his face, other than to say it was not a look I had expected to see on this overconfident, imposing man.

"Call it a case of curiosity. Maybe I wanted to learn more. Let's leave it at that."

Louis, Tassels, and a Website

A public opinion poll from 2016 showed unambiguous support in the US for the farming sector. By an 81 to 15 percent margin, respondents agreed that "a strong and thriving American farm industry is critical to American national security," with 92 percent supporting federal spending to help farmers.[15] Whether this indicates support for farm families or food, I cannot say. As noted earlier, more than 70 percent of Americans say they know nothing or very little about farming or ranching.[16] Whatever support there is in the country for farmers, it is hard to imagine it as running deep given the distance— physical, social, and emotional—the average eater has in relation to this population.

"Detasseling" is a rite of passage for many rural kids in the Midwest. Seed companies contract with farmers, who plant two types of corn—the one with its tassels removed will bear the new hybrid seed. These will become what are called "female" rows; the others, those that will retain their tassels, are the "male" rows, and they do the pollinating. Fields are generally planted with three or four rows of female to every row of male. Machines do the brunt of the work, removing approximately three-fourths of the tassels. The mechanization process is not perfect, however. Stalks are of variable height, with some growing to lengths that increase the likelihood of being missed by a machine's head. This is where human detasselers come into the picture, to remove whatever is missed by the machine. The window to do all of this is pretty tight, between two and three weeks—the perfect summer gig for a teenager looking to make some bank.

Or maybe an opportunity to engender empathy?

In this 2016 experiment, 32 self-identified foodies active in urban food initiatives in Minnesota's Twin Cities—Minneapolis–St. Paul— spent two days detasseling corn. I should also mention that they were all registered Democrats. All of them voted for Obama, those old enough did so both times—2008 and 2012. Participants' ages at the time of the experiment ranged from 23 to 61.

I spend a lot of time around people with an interest in food and find it worrisome how little some know about food production. Not that I am surprised, as the average foodie has never set foot on a farm, save for those located in urban locales and those supplying direct-to-consumer markets—CSA farms, for example. Who are these foodies? I admit that the "foodie" identifier does not mean much anymore, thanks in part to the proliferation of television programs celebrating food, including plenty with a populous feel—for example, *Diners, Drive-Ins and Dives*. Or in other cases food is central to the show but gimmicky, like the hit web series *Hot Ones*—celebrities are interviewed by host Sean Evans while consuming a plate of increasingly spicy chicken wings. A 2019 survey of 2,000 Americans found that more than half, 53 percent to be specific, consider themselves foodies.[17]

If more than half of Americans consider themselves foodies, a figure even higher among those younger than 35, the designation is almost too loose to be meaningful. The individuals enrolled for this experiment shared certain characteristics. This was a passionate and committed group populated by people who *already* considered themselves empathetic and open to difference. None were content watching the rise of the foodie identifier from the outside. As for the food porn you might find on the *Food Network*: "No time for that," one community gardener and food-truck owner-operator told me when asked if, as a chef, he had any interest in watching other chefs on television. All used the term *activist* when describing what they did. This declaration was backed up by action, from protesting inner-city food injustices to working to improve food access for immigrant communities and by their community-oriented volunteerism. Yet for all of their progressive sensibilities, they could not—or they chose not to—understand conventional farmers and rural livelihoods. That same food-truck chef, at the beginning of the experiment, had this to say on the subject: "Why should I give a crap about 'em? Their politics, their large-scale farms, their genetically modified food, their farm subsidies. They're part of the problem." As I said in my introductory chapter, no political party or group has a monopoly on empathy, including those said to be championing it.

This section introduces a pivot that will become a more common theme in the next two chapters: empathy deficits are not a Red or Blue problem but something we all need to take some responsibility for.

The experiment's overall structure looked a lot like that described in the berry boot camp study. Participants were interviewed before and after the experience. A temporary website was developed describing the struggles faced by farmers. There was a page addressing farmer and farm family mental health—did you know that farmer suicides are a major problem in this country?[18] Another click took viewers to a page on rural health care access, or the lack thereof. Rural residents are on average generally older than urban residents. Median age of all people living in rural areas is 43 years, compared with 36 years for urban inhabitants; looking only at adults, those numbers jump to 51 and 45, respectively.[19] Yet I have never met a city dweller who had to drive more than an hour to the nearest hospital, which is a regular fact of life for many nonmetro residents.[20] The website also provided plenty of information about the anxieties attached to farmer and rancher livelihoods. No one wants, for example, to be "the one" who bankrupted the family's namesake in the face of declining commodity prices, skyrocketing farmland values, and the erosion of market power among producers.

The late afternoon heat and humidity draped itself around us like a wet blanket. I had just sat down with Louis. We were relaxing on the front porch of his ranch-style house in a suburb just south of the Twin Cities. The sun, barely above the oak trees to my back, shown directly in his eyes. After the briefest hesitation, he grabbed his hat from the table between us and put it on. Wide-brimmed in tan canvas, the adornment immediately relaxed his grimace, making his face less foreboding.

During our first interview, Louis confessed to "not having a lot of sympathy for those in conventional agriculture." In his words, equating

farm subsidies to corporate welfare, "I have a hard time supporting anyone whose business model requires taking government handouts." He
could not understand why "large-scale farmers get thousands if not
hundreds of thousands of dollars of taxpayer money while those growing food for local markets and vulnerable communities get squat." As
the manager of one of the area's larger urban community gardens, he
was keenly aware of what he called the "great disparity" between federal
rural and urban farm support, an asymmetry that irked him greatly.

Thanks to things like the Freedom of Information Act, we have good
data on the subject. Louis's comments are not uninformed. In recent
years, between 13 and 15 billion dollars in farm subsidies have flowed
to fewer than 1 million recipients.[21] If it were evenly distributed across
this population, we would be looking at each of these farmers receiving
approximately $15,000 annually. Most urban farmers I know could do *a
lot* with that amount. The top 10 farm subsidy recipients have averaged
over the last decade roughly $19 million. Since that is such a large figure,
allow me to break it down into more manageable amounts. That is $1.9
million annually, $158,000 monthly, or $39,580 weekly—a far cry from
the median farm income of roughly $75,000 a year.[22]

Meanwhile, the same type of support for fruit and vegetable production, especially among smaller growers participating in direct-to-
consumer supply chains (CSAs, farmers' markets, etc.), is so small that
it is hard to get accurate figures. According to one study, a paltry 0.5
percent of farm USDA subsidies go toward vegetable, fruit, and nut
growers. In contrast, 80 percent goes to support the growing of corn,
soybeans, grain, and other oil crops, with the remainder supporting
farms raising livestock, dairy, cotton, and tobacco.[23] These figures do
not even take into consideration things like Trump's 2019 $12 billion
bailout of soybean farmers, to soften the economic blow of his trade
war with China. Some farmers, thanks to this bailout, reportedly have
gotten checks from the government totaling $2.8 million.[24]

So, yeah—I get it. I would be pretty pissed too if I were a struggling urban farmer and hearing about paychecks going to my rural peers containing that many digits. But that bitterness is misdirected if you think all commodity growers see those levels of support. The truth of the matter is, most are getting the short end of the stick, too.

That was the Louis I had gotten to know during the first interview. Hypercritical of federal farm policies and their principal beneficiaries, he had little to say that was nice about larger-scale commodity farmers. While still critical of US agricultural policy by the second interview, his hostility to farmers "on the dole"—his words—had dissipated.

"I know—*right?*" he voiced with a slight headshake and smile that conveyed someone in disbelief. He was responding to the question, "Is this the same person who told me two weeks ago that they have no sympathy for conventional farmers?"

Louis had been telling me about how "rural farmers have it tough," adding, "they work their asses off, which you sort of have to respect; they're just trying to keep food on their table." This statement reflects quite a turn of attitude, given his statements a few short weeks prior hammering the population for its dependence on farm subsidies.

"I'd probably do the same," he later confessed, after imagining himself in their shoes and in a situation where farm support was the norm among peers and with commodity and land prices being what they are.

Not long after that, he started in on farmer suicides. "Farmers have the highest suicide rate of any other group—twice the rate among veterans," he told me. I knew the statistics, because I had them on the website that was shared with participants.[25] He admitted to obtaining the information from the emailed hyperlink, along with a lot of other material.

Of the 32 people recruited for this experiment, 15 clicked on the link when first invited, though only five navigated beyond the home page. Those recruited to participate were deeply committed to creating what I would call healthy urban food systems. The group consisted of self-described activists, urban farmers, planners, community organizers, and a dietitian for a school district. Given their backgrounds, I had expected a better response to the website invitation. These were people who claimed to care deeply about food systems. Since when were rural commodity producers not part of that landscape? I get it; they were undoubtedly busy. But who isn't?

Initial interviews helped me understand that underwhelming initial response rate to the website invitation, though they did little to make me feel better about the situation. The attitudes I encountered toward rural commodity producers ranged from ambivalence (e.g., "I don't give rural farmers much thought") to outright hostility (e.g., "I'd be fine if the alternative food movement put them out of business"). This made the response to my second invitation all the more surprising. *One hundred percent* clicked the hotlink when sent the second time, with 30 out of 32 navigating beyond the first page.

Could their time in the field have been responsible for this change, transforming the information the website contained from being noise—what's filtered out—to signal—what is allowed in? For Louis, the answer proved to be *yes*.

Those two days detasseling did not personalize farming, not in the sense we tend to think about process—that "know your farmer" stuff. No surprises there. Everyone met the farm's owners during morning introductions and instructions. But that encounter totaled maybe 20 minutes, and it was more a monologue than a dialogue—not that, again, I think talking is a panacea.

The exercise, rather, connected at other levels.

Rural farmers and urban eaters circle like planets in their own unique orbits, which happen to cross every now and again, but even then, there is no guarantee that the occasion is eventful. As Louis explained, "I've talked with grain farmers at meetings and workshops, but that doesn't mean anything. I talk to a lot of people who I still don't care for."

His comment is an important admission and a useful reminder, namely, about how care for an individual or group may be more a *precondition* for meaningful deliberation than an outcome of it. How, then, do we develop a sense of care for a group if not by talking with them?

"There was something about being out there, of being reminded that farmers are people too and that the lives they've committed themselves to is no cakewalk," he later confessed. "It wasn't—." Louis paused midsentence. I saw a face transformed, looking as morose as my nine-year-old when told to do his homework.

"It wasn't very compassionate, what I said when we first talked," he said, starting softly but building in volume with each word.

Having found his regular speaking voice, he continued: "It was good, helpful, that website; had I not detasseled, I might not have gotten there."

I cannot be sure if the *there* in that comment was a reference to the website or his newfound feelings about farmers. Probably both, which is what makes these findings so encouraging.

Intuitively, it seems easiest to grasp the structure, purpose, and, most important, outcomes of the berry experiment. The link between laboring in the field and the building up of empathy for field laborers seems familiar. Like when I was asked to take care of a bag of flour for a week in high school to get a feel for what it would be like to have a child. I am not suggesting that the experiments are the same or that the former actually works. I am just saying that we are familiar with the idea of how putting yourself in another's shoes might indeed have experiential value. If the detasselers were putting themselves in anyone's shoes it would have been the crocs of pimpled midwestern teenagers—the people that generally do this sort of work, at least in my experience.

This experiment *was* different, though I must confess to still be working through what all those differences were and how they mattered. Unlike the berry study or the SNAP challenge, the detasseling experience is a weak example at best of putting oneself in another's shoes. Maybe there is a lesson in that, namely, that these experiences operate on multiple levels. Some work more directly on *what* one thinks, such as, for instance, by showing just how hard it is to eat on about four dollars a day. Other times, these experiences operate through their effects on secondary cognition—those processes that shape *how* we think.

The experience's tactility mattered: abrasive corn leaves endlessly rubbing against exposed arms, legs, and faces; sore shoulders from keeping one's hands at chest height; the fresh, clean, pleasant smell of Midwest topsoil; the piercing sound of a mosquito in flight that somehow goes from being indiscernible to sounding like it is coming from within one's own head. Each could feel the scale of the . . . well—*everything.*

As Lori put it, "I don't care how big your tractors are, this is *a lot* of ground to be responsible for, which I'm guessing means learning to live with debt and lenders breathing down your neck."

This sounds a lot like something said by Louis. When asked to reflect on what he learned from detasseling, he referenced the "enormity of it all" and, later, "the isolation"—descriptors, in my experience, rarely applied in the absence of immediate perception. His was a fitting response, an honest statement of what he knows, a familiarity, that he did not know prior. But his learning did not end there. That act of primary cognition appears to have also shaped how he thought, as evidenced by him being drawn toward that information on the website that he earlier ignored and this, collectively, changing his prior antipathy for conventional farmers to something more akin to empathy.

Combating Indifference

It was the second day of fieldwork. The briefest of rain showers had passed through overnight, leaving the uppermost crust of the topsoil moist and leaves wet. The evening low momentarily dropped to 75 degrees with the rain but rebounded quickly. The leaves of the corn remained moist for most of the morning thanks to the humidity. The day was shaping up to be another hot one.

Stephanie had come to embrace the stereotypes thrown at her over the years. "I'm a proud, super crunchy activist. I've been called 'hippy.' I've also been called a lot worse. It's all good; I don't get caught up with labels."

She wore well-kept dreadlocks and was dressed in tan shorts and a red shirt, though her sleeve tattoos gave the effect of wearing layers. Her aura had a unique captivating quality to it. She had an expressive personality that was helped by a strong voice that was at the same time soft. It reminded me of a goose-down feather—airy around the edges but with a stout, penetrating core. Taken on the whole, she had one of those presences whose absence created an immediate want.

Stephanie spent much of her 20s WWOOFing. Volunteers for World Wide Opportunities on Organic Farms—WWOOF: pronounced "woof," like what a dog says[26]—travel (typically) to lower-income countries and work on organic farms in exchange for food and accommodation. In that capacity, Stephanie had worked on farms in India, Nigeria, and Ghana. Yet when asked whether she had labored on anything other than an *urban* farm in the US, she gave me one of those hand-caught-in-the-cookie-jar grins. The face said it without help from the lips: *Busted!*

She licked her lips, which had the effect of wiping the expression from view, before explaining, "Naw I haven't. Ridiculous, right? But I'm here now. Better late than never."

Unlike some in the group, Stephanie was not initially inimical to large-scale conventional growers. She was indifferent, yes, but not hostile. I am not sure, however, if indifference is really any better than hostility, certainly not when recalling the words of the Nobel Laureate, and Holocaust survivor, Elie Wiesel: "Indifference elicits no response. Indifference is not a response. Indifference is not a beginning; it is an end. And, therefore, indifference is always the friend of the enemy, for it benefits the aggressor—never his victim, whose pain is magnified when he or she feels forgotten."[27]

I realize it might be controversial in some circles to cast farmers as victims. Agriculture has been roundly criticized, and rightly so, for locking-in white privilege at multiple levels.[28] According to one survey, individuals who identify as white own 98 percent of all farmland nationally.[29] Even urban farmers' markets have been dinged by critical food scholars for being overly homogeneous and feeding people based on how all those farmers from European decent eat—called "eating whiteness" in the literature.[30] Meanwhile, setting race and ethnic identity to the side, the USDA places the average (rural) farm income at roughly $75,000 annually, which is a good bit higher than the national nonfarm average—approximately $60,000.[31] While I would not suggest that this is evidence of farmer privilege, it does illustrate that there are far worse paying occupations. Just look to the other "end" of the food system, and you'll find some of them. Full-time food preparation and serving workers, including fast-food employees, average about $22,000 annually.[32]

It was the end of the second day. Stephanie was sitting on the opened tailgate of an F-150 pickup, changing out of tennis shoes and into sandals. Approaching from her left, I saw the smile immediately. "What are you grinning about?" I asked when the distance separating us no longer necessitated yelling.

She looked up, surprised, confessing as much, "Didn't think anyone was around. I was just thinking."

She proceeded to tell me about her time WWOOFing, noting that the experience involved living with farmers for weeks and in one instance seven months. "Not surprisingly, it had a huge impact on how I thought about that group"—*that group* being smaller-scale organic farmers in other parts of the world.

She continued, "I don't know how someone wouldn't be changed when immersed in another world like that." She had a look on her face that told me she was building to something important, or at least to something that she felt held importance.

"This was a totally different experience," she pointed out, adding, "I mean, we were just picking off tassels; scratching the surface of what it means to farm, really."

With that her eyes turned to the field, as if looking for what to say among the green leaves. She resumed with a voice that held a new element of resolve.

"It really begs the question, 'Do you have to be immersed in a lifestyle to understand it, or at least to appreciate it?' Maybe not. I can tell you that I have never thought more about conventional corn farmers than I have over these two days."

She then asked, "Do I know what it means to be a large-scale corn farmer because of this experience?" The question was directed to no one in particular, though she took it upon herself to answer.

"No, of course not. But I can't say I'm as indifferent about this group as I once was."

On more cynical days, I might be inclined to be suspicious that that experience was responsible for explaining what I was hearing. But even then, I'd remind myself that it was not only the experience but also the website—a one-two epistemic combo.

At one point that morning she quipped, referencing things said in public forums held in the Twin Cities on food access and neighbor-level food security, "Stuff comes out of my mouth that sounds insensitive to those who grow things like corn and soybeans. Tearing others down to lift others up isn't helpful."

I was also struck by how she offered these admissions. Her otherwise unfailing voice had more than once that morning not held true. During those moments her words sounded raspy and uncertain. She sounded like a person displaying elements of . . . well, remorse.

I began to probe for an explanation of Stephanie's newfound empathy.

"Yeah, I did. Seemed like the right thing to do given what I experienced that day." This was Stephanie's response to being asked if she dug out my first email to the group, the one with the hyperlink. She had visited my website the night prior. The tell was that she quoted a statistic about the rural-urban digital divide, namely, the one about how 97 percent of Americans in urban areas have access to high-speed internet whereas in rural areas that number is only 65 percent.[33]

Recall earlier when I wrote about how this experiment was different from the berry study. Its links to the headland, *by way of the heartland*, represent an important observation. Again, according to Stephanie, visiting the website "seemed like the right thing to do given what I experienced that day." The antecedent is clear in that sentence.

Treatments of empathy take many forms. Yet we can quickly assess their implications by their ability to overcome indifference, which is the first step to caring. And this begins the process of recognition: to view rural, large-scale commodity farmers neither as victims nor as people of privilege but as individuals with legitimate concerns, aspirations, and fears.

→ CHAPTER 6 ←

Urban-Rural Food Plans

MOST OF THE STORIES I have told until this point have been derived from experiments of my own creation. This chapter is unusual in the sense that it pulls principally from natural experiments that I have had the good fortune to be part of. But before going into that, I want to review data from research that has taken me to all sixty-four of Colorado's counties.

Remember that the encounters being encouraged can take multiple forms and need not be as contrived as, say, the SNAP challenge or berry boot camp. The prior experiments could be repeated in a variety of institutions—schools, clubs, places of worship. I want to suggest with this chapter that we can also think bigger. Could supply chains be reimagined to deliver on enhancing rural and urban livelihoods while also engendering compassion and care among those involved?

But first, some stage setting . . .

"Oh, you have to drive 40 miles, over that mountain, if you want that." We have all had "aha!" moments, when a revelation surprises us with insight. By the look on his face, I was bearing witness to its outward expression.

I was visiting southern Colorado, conducting interviews in one of the state's 23 "frontier" counties. The term is used by the US government to describe any county with a population density of six or fewer persons per square mile. At that particular moment, the person doing the talking was a school administrator. He was telling us about broadband access or, more accurately, the district's lack thereof. Joining me on this interview was Joshua, an ambitious 23-year-old who had spent all but the last four months of his life in Chicago and its ritzy north shore area. We were being told about the limits of dial-up internet for delivering online course content. Learning that teachers preload low-resolution videos ahead of time, Joshua had blurted out, "How do you watch Netflix?"

The 40-mile-drive reference was the response.

Fortunately, things are getting better. By urging state agencies to create grants to fund internet infrastructure, helping communities apply for that money, and facilitating partnerships, the Colorado Broadband Office (CBO)—the fact that the state has such an office is telling—has done an admirable job closing the broadband gap in the state. Since the office began collecting data in 2015, rural access to broadband has improved from 59 to 87 percent.[1] COVID brought these inequities into particularly stark relief, especially when the governor issued a statewide stay-at-home order in early 2020. This contrast includes the broadband *sometimers* as much as the broadband *have nots*—just because a rural community has high-speed internet does not mean it was built to handle every child learning from home, a great many adults working from their kitchen tables, and a statewide shift toward telehealth.

The school I was standing in was part of that 13 percent without broadband. "Streaming" refers in these parts to something that happens after a downpour or what ranchers do when nature calls, not something you do with your television or phone.

Joshua had never lived anywhere in want of high download speeds. I could tell what he was thinking before he said it. The sentiment was spread across his face and eyes. "To think that people live like that—inconceivable."

It is inconceivable. And that is the problem.

How many Americans really know what it is like to live in the countryside, recognizing that more than 80 percent of the US population lives in urban areas?[2] Sure, many of those come for a visit. But the rural communities visited by the 80-plus percent tend to be amenity rich in one form or another. They have bed and breakfasts, antique stores, multiple restaurants, Airbnb listings, quaint cafés . . . oh, and high-speed internet. The "other" rural America, the one urban Americans rarely visit, is as distant for many as another country—the one they *think* they know from movies and television, with the crotch-scratching, overall-wearing imbecile standing among his derelict automobiles.

This is all to say, I was not surprised by Joshua's reaction. To be honest, I brought him along hoping for such a revelation. This interview was one out of hundreds that I have conducted in Colorado between 2012 and 2018.

My methodological philosophy is a mixed bag. Interviews are typically semi-structured, which is lingo in qualitative research circles to say that while I always have a game plan, I don't always follow it. I also like trying new things when gathering data, a practice born of necessity more than anything else. A major methodological challenge for all the sciences, as I see it, is grasping and making sense of those elements of the world that cannot be easily reduced to words or numbers. The 20th-century philosopher of science, Paul Feyerabend, reveled in the sensory and intellectual abundance that surrounds us, which we can only know in fits and starts, especially in the social sciences. ("This is a blessing, not a drawback," he wrote, adding, "a superconscious organism would not be superwise, it would be paralyzed.")[3] Take the concept of empathy: how do you know it when you see it?

One example of this methodological experimentation comes from this statewide study. Within my semi-structured survey instrument was the question, "What most contributes to one reaching their fullest potential: society, community, or the individual?" Respondents were then handed a pen and paper with an image of a triangle. Each point on the triangle was identified by one of the following three options: society, community, and individual. With the triangle in hand, they were asked to "identify with a dot the location on the image that best represents your answer to the question"—the thinking being that most people would not approach the question in either/or terms but with a degree of nuance. They were then asked to repeat the task: "But this time answer as you think someone would from an alternative metropolitan/nonmetropolitan classification." With this question, I was interested in how well those interviewed could place themselves in the shoes of someone from the other "end" of the metropolitan continuum. Dot locations were then converted to data points and fed into heat-map software. (A heat map displays data by assigning a shade to individual values. Typically, deeper colors signify great intensity of values.) Figures 6.1a–c consist of 264 individual data points, made up of responses from interviewees located in urban (n = 114), rural (n = 107), and frontier (n = 45) counties.[4]

Answers from those in urban areas show greatest intensity near the "top," privileging "society." Those from rural counties gave responses that landed lower on the image, closer to and equidistant from "the individual" and "community" points. Finally, those from frontier counties saw their answers group closer to the "community" corner.

Part of my motivation for engaging respondents in this exercise involved wanting to explore elements pointing to how they think the world *is* and *ought* to be, realizing these outlooks profoundly shape one's politics.[5] I also wanted to see if there was any truth to talking about rural and urban folks not seeing eye to eye about things. I say

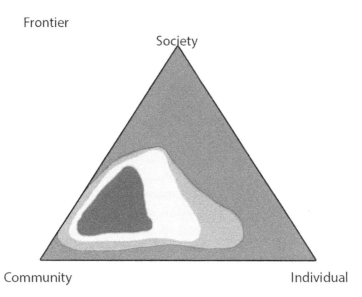

FIGURE 6.1A   Frontier county responses.

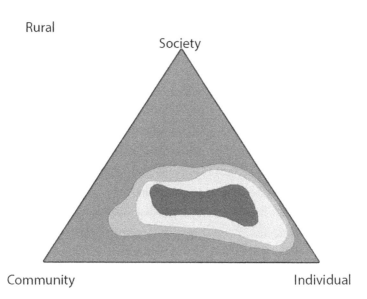

FIGURE 6.1B   Rural county responses.

Urban

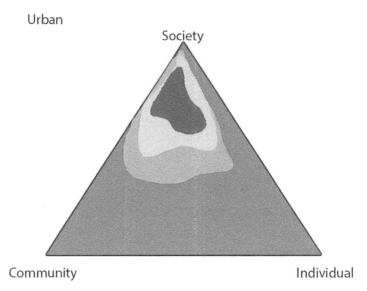

FIGURE 6.1C   Urban county responses.

that also realizing, of course, that there is nothing monolithic about any of these groups—geography is not destiny.

I have presented these images on numerous occasions. The question I get the most is, "Why would respondents living in frontier counties place more importance on 'community' than those from rural counties?" A fair query in light of the classic image of these people: one of rugged individualism. Have a look at almost any pickup truck advertisement—hint: they're not selling socialism. Not coincidentally, states with the highest statewide market share of new vehicle purchases that are pickups generally vote Republican; in Wyoming and North Dakota, for instance, almost half of new autos bought are trucks.[6]

Jerry was a rancher living in the far northwest corner of the state in a frontier county. He explained his dot placement this way: "This is God's Country. But look around, there are no hospitals in heaven, no stores, no repair shops, no contractors, no plumbers, no tutors or babysitting agencies."

With sleeves rolled to elbows resting against the top of a closed tailgate connected to his ever-dusty Ford F-350, Jerry continued, though his tone had changed. It sounded more defiant, or maybe a better word is *determined*. "Family, friends and neighbors, that's what you have out here—*community*."

He stared at me steely eyed, and I remember nodding reflexively. Apparently satisfied with my response, he added, "You've got to be independent out here, but there's no way you can thrive without the support of others." He then pointed around the ranch while offering statements about the team efforts that went into making it all work. From rebuilt transmissions to repaired fencing, reroofed homes, the installation of hot-water heaters, even childbirth, the fingerprints of members from the community were all around.

The truth of the matter is, the individualist/collectivist dichotomy is as much a Western construct as the headland model of attitudinal and behavioral change. Have you honestly ever met anyone who operates according to purely egoistic self-interest? Scholars who study this stuff for a living, including a few studies by yours truly, have shown that even individuals who exhibit so-called individualistic values still regularly put group needs ahead of their own.[7] This likely never rises to the level of global cosmopolitanism, where the "us" being cared for is both broad and abstract—this is your prototypical global citizen.[8] The point, however, is that even so-called individualists have it in them to think about others in a caring and compassionate way.

This is an important realization because it shows the individualist/collectivist dichotomy is overblown. We all value certain groups. It's just a matter of expanding the tent. The challenge before us lies in knowing that getting people to alter those deep cultural values is hard, at least from a headland's standpoint.

The triangles are also telling about the current state of things from the perspective of detailing a gap between *perceptions* of how others think and *reality*. On this point, note the responses when individuals were asked to put themselves in the shoes of someone from an alternative metropolitan classification. When asked to respond as a "typical rural resident would," urban residents overwhelmingly missed the mark, placing the dot near the corner designated "the individual." Meanwhile, nonmetropolitan residents—those from both rural and frontier counties—performed no better, believing urban residents on the whole held collectivist-type outlooks. Jerry's response was typical for this group: "City folks—hell, they're all a bunch of socialists." Before discarding that outlook as the ravings of some close-minded country bumpkin, realize such outlandish characterizations cut both ways, as evidenced by when someone from Denver informed me that "the average rural voter operates by a leave-me-the-hell-alone-to-do-whatever-I-want political philosophy."

I started this book noting that empathy starts not by changing minds but by changing our opinions of others. Add to that the need to also change our opinion of others' opinions. Stereotypes take all forms.

When Physical Segregation Is Part of the Equation

In the book *The Space Between Us*, political scientist Ryan Enos explores the ways that social geography creates walls.[9] He notes the strong correlation between support for Trump in the 2016 election and a community's growing Latino population. Elaborating on this relationship in an interview, referring to the 2016 presidential election, Enos says, "The more recent growth in Latino population, the more likely white non-Latinos were to vote for Trump. Much of this was driven by white Democrats, presumably who voted for Obama, now voting for Trump."[10]

Rural View of Urban

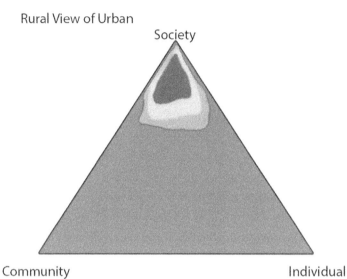

FIGURE 6.2A   Rural and frontier view of urban inhabitants.

Urban View of Rural

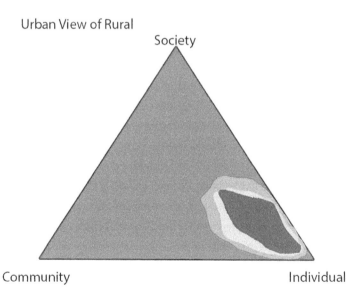

FIGURE 6.2B   Urban view of rural and frontier inhabitants.

Newly diverse communities in the US also tend to be highly segregated. Levels of segregation in a community have been shown to be positively correlated with discriminatory attitudes and practices toward nonwhites.[11] The solution, or at least one of them, is interpersonal contact, which Enos describes as "the antidote for geographically-based division," adding, "people come together in cities to do things like work, go to sporting events, lobby government, and so on, and they have contact with the other groups doing the same thing."[12] Urban spaces can be built to foster these connections. Strategies to do this might include mixed-use development, public transportation that connects diverse neighborhoods, and the creation of welcoming and accessible public spaces, like outdoor markets, parks, and community gardens.

Great suggestions, save for one important fact: they do not translate well for overcoming rural-urban divisions, a reference to populations who will *always* be physically segregated. I know some people in Colorado who live more than 200 miles from the nearest city—if 12,000 people constitute a "city." If your definition looks something more like Denver, then those people are facing a 400-mile drive, slowed by a couple of 10,000-plus feet mountain passes, *each way*.

This brings me to the subject of urban food policy plans.

Residents of cities of all sizes—some with fewer than 50,000 people, others with populations in the millions—are thinking hard about issues around food procurement, distribution, and consumption. Worldwide, 211 cities, totaling roughly half a billion people, have signed the Milan Urban Food Policy Pact (MUFPP), a commitment to work for more equitable, just, and sustainable urban food systems.[13] (The pact was launched in October 2015 and led by the mayor of Milan, Italy. It represents the first international protocol through which city leaders commit to developing sustainable food systems to grant healthy and accessible food to all, protect biodiversity, and fight food waste. The most recent US signatory, as of October 2020, is New Port Richey, Florida, joining the pact in July 2020.)[14] Many more municipalities are following their own paths, creating policies to drive food system–based investments and food-consumption goals, such as by directing procurement within their publicly funded institutions (schools, prisons, hospitals, etc.) or through public-private partnerships.[15]

Yet as with any urban policy, farmers and rural communities are not well represented, by which I mean, *not at all* represented. I get it: urban politicians and city-funded urban institutions do not exist to serve someone not among their electorate or who does not contribute, via local taxes, to the city's coffers.

Nevertheless, we are missing an opportunity here.

The city of Denver has 12 farms, totaling 129 acres, according to the 2017 Census of Agriculture, down from the 27 farms (609 acres) recorded 10 years prior. (Curiously, it gained two farms since the 2012 census but *lost* 14 total acres under cultivation.) In 2015, the City and County of Denver began developing its first long-term strategic vision for the future of food in the city and county. The Denver City Council and the Mayor's Office supported the development of a comprehensive, citywide food plan to bring about greater alignment across the wide range of stakeholders. The resulting document, the Denver Food Vision and Plan, emerged from a public engagement process that generated a total of 4,918 comments from 22 listening sessions and focus groups. Goals in the plan include having "25 percent of all food purchased by public institutions come from Colorado" and "$100 million of new capital to Denver food businesses."[16]

There's a move afoot to be intentional with Denver's Food Vision and Plan and others like it in surrounding metro communities. By that I mean there is a desire by parties throughout the state, private and public, metro and nonmetro, to find ways to have cities meet their food plan goals while building supply chains that reach out to the very rural communities that feel ignored, no thanks in part to how urban food plans are usually designed and implemented. I have talked with many of these individuals and been in spaces where these thorny subjects are discussed. It is one thing to *say* the goal is to create rural-urban links through food and entirely another thing to actually *do* it.

I reflect below on my experiences in this project, involving motivated partisans of all persuasions. Again, that's the beauty of food. We tend to project what we want to see in the concept. Thanks to this high polysemy, talk of a food plan was enough to bring wildly different groups together, at least for long enough to start something.

Good Food, Bad Farmers

Paige is a registered dietician nutritionist and the Nutrition and Menu Specialist for a metropolitan school district in the greater Denver area. She is a respected nutritional health professional who also happens to be well-connected. Her closest neighbor is her district's representative in state government. Her regular golfing partners include the city manager of a nearby community and an area school district superintendent. Not surprisingly, when her community of some 100,000 souls set out to create a "food policy framework"—that's what she called it: a document setting guiding principles for local food investments and public-institution procurement goals—the powers that be sought Paige's input and involvement.

We met at an outdoor café in a park of her suburban neighborhood, a mature community. The trees around and above dripped with life, their budding branches days away from erupting with leaves to suckle the sun. Spring. The scent of organic material was enough to remind us of our immediate surroundings, while the whiffs of exhaust and sounds of traffic coming from the nearby boulevard made it impossible to forget what lay beyond.

About a year prior—this would have been early 2017—Paige was part of a panel on childhood obesity in the state. Though frequently lauded as the fittest state in the union, with sedentary and obesity rates at roughly 15 percent and 20 percent, respectively (the national average obesity rate is closer to 35 percent), there has been a notable uptick in childhood obesity rates in recent years.[17] Also on the panel and in the audience were farmers from around the state.

"I mentioned the importance of eating fresh fruits and vegetables in our community's plan and was immediately, and later I would admit *rightfully*, challenged."

The most vocal challenge came from the Colorado potato growers in the room. Colorado is the second-largest potato-growing region in the US, with most coming from the San Luis Valley—the largest alpine valley on the planet. The first person at a microphone during the Q&A segment of the panel was a potato grower from this southern region of the state. He was there to tell Paige that some varieties of potatoes are every bit as healthy as any leafy green.

"He was gripping the microphone, obliviously upset. His knuckles were white, I swear," she explained with a flinty glare and determined jaw that told me she was not easily intimidated.

"He ended up being right, you know," she confessed, adding, "Health professionals like myself like to demonize the potato when, as I've since learned, some have incredible micronutrient profiles. So: yeah—some are every bit as healthy as the leafy greens we're always pushing."

It might sound a bit awkward to say farmers feel shame in how people like Paige talk about what good food looks like. It is not a term they would use to describe how they feel either, though many would agree that they believe the people behind most urban food policy plans are *shaming* their rural way of life. I do not mean to call Paige out, as if what she said somehow ran counter to the rhetoric typically batted about in spaces where issues of urban food procurement are discussed.

Eliot's family has grown potatoes in the San Luis Valley since William McKinley lived in the White House. We last saw each other in 2019. That particular event brought together Colorado farmers with those in the greater-Denver area who set its food policy and make procurement decisions for its schools and prisons. Someone from the City of Denver had just finished a presentation on their Denver Food Vision and Plan. The talk ended by discussing the Good Food Purchasing Program—a program of great interest to many institutions along the Front Range. First adopted by the City of Los Angeles and the LA Unified School District in 2012, the Good Food Purchasing Program helps institutions across the country, with its metric-based standards, acquire food that is, well—*good*. Goals of the program include food procurement that supports local economies, provides safe and healthy working conditions and fair compensation for workers across the supply chain, enhances environmental sustainability, and ensures animal welfare. For an example of how these standards are operationalized, note their aim of supporting local economies, which, as stated on their website, "is based on a combination of farm size (by acreage) and farm distance from purchasing institution (based on driving distance)."[18]

We were sitting together at the back of the room against a round table. Though the table held only the two of us, we had scooched together so we could see the stage. We were close enough that I could smell the Listerine on his breath whenever he leaned toward my ear. Displeased with what he had just heard, he apparently could not wait until we had left our seats to vent.

"You know what good food means to these guys? Food from small farms within a 100-mile radius that's organic." Pausing long enough to place a hand on his chest, he added, "I guess that means the food coming from a larger farm that's been around for more than a century doesn't produce good food." Losing the whispered-tone, he blurted out loud enough for other tables to hear, "They're basically saying I'm not a good farmer. How can I be one, if my food isn't deemed good in their eyes?"

Political economists talk about a *moral* economy to highlight that "all economic institutions are founded on norms defining rights and responsibilities that have legitimations (whether reasonable or unreasonable), require some moral behavior of actors, and generate effects that have ethical implications."[19] Which is to say, markets, *all* markets, enforce and are premised on beliefs of the "good" and "right," ethical outlooks that are not always—heck, more like *never*—agreed on by impacted parties. That is what incensed Paige's potato-growing antagonists, namely, that *their* beliefs about what constitutes good food were not being respected. This was taken as a personal affront. *They're basically saying I'm not a good farmer.*

It has been said that an injury is much sooner forgotten than an insult.[20] And we wonder why some rural constituents in the state feel left behind—11 counties in Colorado tried, unsuccessfully, to secede from the other 53 in 2013 to become a separate state.

Paige's relationship with this group has since improved considerably.

The Good Food Purchasing Program came up at one point during our chat in the park. Once a diehard supporter of the program, she has since come to question the moral economies the program looks to enact.

"Some of it had to do with being exposed to different facts. The growers sat me down and schooled me on potato varieties that might one day become the next 'super food,'" she explained straight-faced, indicating an acceptance of relinquishing the title of "expert" to trusted potato farmers on matters of nutrition relating to tubers.

Wanting to hear more, I asked, "You said, 'some of it had to do with being exposed to different facts,' which suggests other things were also at work to get you to change your position. *Such as?*"

She straightened up and looked forward. Straight-ahead was a curious juxtaposition between the stationary, textured trees and the shiny traffic rushing just beyond. She closed her eyes and breathed deeply. A second or two passed before her eyes opened with a start, as if realizing only then that it was her turn to speak.

"It's hard to *say*," she started. Reducing heartland experiences to words can be difficult. "What I mean—it's just that, I visited some of their farms and got to experience firsthand how things operate. Many of these farms have deep roots in their communities, you know."

What Paige eventually got around to saying was that those personal encounters made her want to find facts to support her newly acquired desire to assist potato growers. "You couldn't help but want to find ways to justify incorporating potatoes into my community's food plan," is how she explained landing where she did. This was after acquiring immediate experience about potato-reliant rural economies. During one such visit, she talked to someone at a gas station and learned how the farm she visited was single-handedly responsible for keeping the local library in the black.

Big Hair, Bolo Ties, and Unseemly Odors

Bias and prejudice come in all forms. This doesn't mean it exists at equal levels in all of those variants. Some forms are unquestionably more egregious than others. But I do think it is important, when talking about issues of inclusivity and bias, that we call out intolerance whenever it presents itself, which includes prejudice toward rural people, places, and cultural practices. Research has shown, for example, that people who list listening to country music among their hobbies on job applications are less likely to get an interview for white-collar positions compared to those reporting activities such as sailing.[21] Pivoting to agriculture, we know that farmers—even white, educated, male ones—suffer as a result of their identities, often *because of* rather than despite their performances of white heteromasculinity.[22] Responding to a sense of duty, the men in these roles have been known to stay behind to keep family farms going, while younger siblings leave in search of greener pastures. Even the language of "staying behind" implies for some a sense of failure and exclusion, while those getting away talk of having "escaped."[23] We know, too, that rural residents face taunts in their performance of rurality, which they may express through dress, mannerisms, or hobbies. I am not suggesting these affronts rise to the moral equivalent of a black person being called the n-word. But that doesn't make those put-downs sting any less. I have documented some of these insults elsewhere, of rural Coloradoans being heckled with terms like *bubba*, *red neck*, and *coowwboyee*—drawn-out, in an exaggerated southern accent.[24]

Antonio has a rich and varied background in the Denver local-food scene. Included among the hats he has worn are urban gardener, food bank volunteer, restaurant owner, farmers' market manager, and activist; the last role got him arrested on a couple of occasions protesting swanky development projects in his long-fought struggle against citywide gentrification. I got to know Antonio a few years back. He was a friend of a friend who invited us both to the grand opening of a Denver-area restaurant that prioritized hiring ex-cons.

An otherwise loving and warm individual who talks regularly about the importance of inclusivity, Antonio held a real disdain for rural folks and their ways of life, "with their guns, trucks, big hair—and even bigger belt buckles—and their bolo ties." I would rather not describe someone who had devoted their life to social justice issues as bigoted, so let me just say he was incredibly close-minded about those from the state's *other* 47 counties—those Coloradoans from a nonmetro zip code.

I got to know Antonio pretty well since our introduction. The above quote about big hair and bolo ties, variations on which have been shared with me on multiple occasions, came out about a year into our friendship, triggered by my pushing him to rethink those prejudices. I should have known better—of course, telling him to not be so close-minded was not going to accomplish anything positive.

In early 2018, Antonio began an involvement that brought him into the same room with growers representing numerous commodity groups—wheat growers, potato farmers, orchardists, ranchers, and sweet-corn producers, just to name a few. His interaction with Colorado farmers and ranchers, save for urban growers, up until that point, had been for all intents and purposes nonexistent. Yet because the events were billed as being about improving food security statewide, and not about rural and urban folks hashing out their differences, Antonio participated willingly and openly, albeit with some degree of initial trepidation.

I unexpectedly ran into Antonio on my campus—Colorado State University—in August 2019. The new academic term was still a week away, but the sidewalks in and around the campus's main spine were congested with anxious students, some still with their parents in tow. Standing at my office door, unannounced, he asked, "Want to grab a coffee?"

He was on campus, about an hour early, to attend a lecture and panel about perennial crops—the exact title escapes me, but it was along the lines of, "Perennial crop solutions to annual agricultural challenges." (Perennial crops are alive year-round and are harvested multiple times before dying, like strawberries, grapes, alfalfa, and asparagus.) One of the panelists had experimented with perennial grains. Antonio had befriended her during one of those Colorado-based rural-urban supply-chain-linking events.

Coffees in hand, we found some well-shaded outdoor seating. Having apprised the other of what each had been up to, the conversation turned to the reason for Antonio's appearance that day.

He had made some new friends since our paths last crossed: that perennial grain producer from the eastern plains, a rancher from the northwestern corner of the state, a potato grower from the San Luis Valley, and a peach farmer from the Western Slope—west of Denver, just beyond the Rocky Mountains. They all make it a point to visit with Antonio when in the Denver-area, and he, in turn, tries to get out to see each of them, *in situ*, annually. Yeah, calling them friends seems like a fair description.

"*Have* I changed? I suppose you could say that." His sarcasm was thick, but there was pain underneath the playfulness. Antonio was responding to my statement-like query, "Look at you. Best friends with farmers. You've changed."

Antonio looked like he wanted to say more. I blew on my coffee and took a few tentative sips, buying him the time needed to figure out what—or how much—to say next.

"They're good people," he explained in the way you say something to yourself in affirmation of a truth you like hearing stated out loud. "It was a struggle at first, thinking we had *anything* in common. Somehow, we found a way to connect."

Antonio struggled to identify how he connected with the ways of life he earlier disparaged—*Somehow, we found a way to connect.* But as he talked about his experiences with these new friends, he left me a zigzagging trail of empirical breadcrumbs. It was enough to allow me to reconstruct his journey to the heartland. One involved the 13-hour roundtrip car ride to central Kansas, coupled with two nights of camping, to an annual event on perennial agriculture with the aforementioned perennial grain expert. Antonio dropped this large crumb when he said, "In addition to learning a lot, there's something downright humanizing when you're that close to someone for such an extended period of time."

Or take his comment about a trip to his friend's ranch in northwestern Moffat County. "To stand in the middle of grasslands that have evolved with the herd. You can't *not* be moved by all that."

A Reminder of Food's Ambivalence

In addition to showing how food can create affordances that connect and engender empathy, this chapter reminds us that food cuts both ways. Think how often we attach a normative modifier to the word *food*: *good, junk, authentic, all-natural,* and so forth. That has consequences, which go well beyond amending the noun. Other terms regularly used to describe food might not be explicitly normative, but we treat them as though they were, terms like *organic, local, free range,* and *GMO-free.* Yet many of these ethical foods come from some of the biggest corporate players in the food system, as evidenced by, for instance, Walmart's presence as the largest organic retailer in North America, followed by Costco, Kroger, and Target.[25] This explains Julie Guthman's pointed criticism of what she calls the "facile dichotomies between fast and slow, reflexive and compulsive, fat and thin, and, hence, good and bad eaters." A careful analysis will show, she continues, "slippage and instability in these [ethical] categories."[26]

Ethical eating is also shameful, though not in the way you might initially think. I discussed in a prior chapter how the normative weight of a term like *junk food* can weigh negatively on the self-worth of lower-income parents who see the occasional Twinkie or Kool-Aid drink box as an affordable way to treat their children while giving them some semblance of normalcy—a break from being one of *those kids,* always wearing, and otherwise eating, off-brand labels. Similarly, to call some food "good" implies those lacking this designation are "bad." That also pertains to those growing it. If your livelihood rests on growing bad food—or worse, *non*-food, as many of my conventional corn farming friends are charged with doing—what does that make you? I have yet to meet a farmer who grows food for traditional, longer-supply chains who does not take it personally when hearing others decry the evils of conventionally raised crops and livestock. They hate it because to speak ill of those foods is to speak ill of *them*.

I raise this point here because most urban food plans do little to make rural residents, farmers and ranchers in particular, feel like they matter. I am not saying those in nonmetropolitan areas bear no responsibility for this sense of lacking. Nor am I suggesting that the type of encounters I have witnessed working with Colorado growers and urban food policy decision makers go one-way, with urban folks becoming more empathetic toward rural livelihoods while those in the latter category remain unmoved.

I remember in particular my meetings with Craig, a wheat farmer located an hour east of Denver. During one of our more recent visits—ours is a friendship that goes back years—we chatted about the growth taking place in communities a short drive west of his 1,000-plus-acre farm.

His clean-shaven crown and face accentuated protruding cheekbones and a Kirk Douglas chin. The Front Range, the populous region west of Craig's farm running north and south of Denver, is one of the fastest growing in the country.[27] We were meeting so that I could learn more about his experiences supplying metropolitan area schools within this corridor with fresh vegetables and organic wheat.

"The schools can look very different," a nod to the fact that some schools focus on teaching a second or third language, while others might emphasize the arts or sciences. Strip those specializations away and you are left with one constant: all kids have to eat.

I had known Craig a long time, almost 12 years at the time of this interview. When we first met, he was a conventional wheat farmer. Shortly thereafter, he transitioned his land to organic. He added vegetable crops in 2015.

My first interview with Craig all those years ago involved examining his position as a farmer whose operation was in transition to organic certified wheat. Digging through those old transcripts, I came across the following quote that provided a baseline—some preexposure data before he started selling regularly to metropolitan institutions. We were discussing in this decade-old interview the distances he traveled to take his grain to market. What used to be a short 15-minute one-way trip for his grandparents, to the nearest town, was now two hours.

"You go to Denver. They have God-damn Walgreens, banks, and mattress stores at every corner. Their infrastructure, every part of it, is overbuilt." Even though a transcript, you could sense the contrast coming. "Meanwhile, *our* infrastructure is in disrepair. It's a gut punch, paying state taxes that aren't supporting the local economy here."

Fast-forward to 2018, to Craig admitting, "I've got no problem with some of my tax money going to support urban school districts and infrastructure projects in and around Denver."

Why the change of heart? Craig's introduction to urban-facing supply chains seems to have played a role. Yet what really moved Craig was not his participation in markets but the encounters that came with those transactions.

"I went to the schools, visited with the students and administrators; some also came here to visit my farm," Craig explained, adding, "It wasn't that I heard something that I hadn't already been told but that it finally got through to me." The look on my face no doubt conveyed the expectation that I wanted to hear more. Gratefully, he obliged.

"I get it now: perhaps urban municipalities and people aren't much better off, that rather than viewing those in cities as the enemy they ought to be understood as partners. We're all fighting the same fight—globalization, billionaires rigging the system to benefit them[selves], corporate control of our food system."

Another way to think about the encounters described by Craig would be to say that they went beyond being transactional. This is a description of an exchange that leaves participants fundamentally unchanged. Think: "Would you like fries with that?"—a ubiquitous transaction that not only fails to build conviviality or empathy but that can actually lead to socially deleterious outcomes as it habituates the view that others are there to be used. What Craig described being part of instead were *transformative* experiences. Or at least they had the potential to be.

The people Craig got to know in these encounters were more than consumers or potential customers. They had self-worth, as opposed to being viewed purely for their purchasing value.

I wanted to try to experience what Craig experienced—to see if I could see, and ultimately report on, the type of experiences he had had that led him to finally "get it." With that aim in mind, I asked if I could tag along either for his next school visit or for the next busload of kids to his farm. I did not have to wait long: a group of fourth graders was due at his farm in exactly a week.

I got there late, after the bus had arrived. Once within earshot of the group, I could hear Craig talking about how baking flour is made. It was like that for most of the visit. Following the group around for those two hours, I noticed that Craig did most of the talking. Yes, the nine- and ten-year-olds in attendance asked plenty of questions, from "How big is an acre" to "How many cats do you have?" But as far as dialogue goes, things were pretty one-sided. Craig did most of the telling. From a headlands point of view, the information flow was exclusively unidirectional.

But that is not how the event *felt*. Learners were we all, including myself.

The practice of qualitative research has been likened to a dance, at least by the more phenomenologically inclined practitioners: for example, "Researcher and participant thus engage in a dance, moving in and out of experiencing and reflection while simultaneously moving through the shared intersubjective space that is the research encounter."[28] I am choosing to do something a bit different here, using my own experiences to amplify points made by Craig, realizing that I inhabited the space every bit as much as any of the other bodies present that day.

"Did you see those faces? So much laughter. And the smiles. There's just something about having them here."

I waited until the kids were having snacks before approaching Craig and asking for impressions of that day, the query that provoked the prior quote. He went on to tell me things I had heard many times before, like the by-then-familiar comment about the importance of being able to put an "actual face, from an *actual person*, on something." It wasn't particularly clear what that *something* was, as the inflection came immediately after the comment about the laughing, smiling children. He could have been talking, say, about taxes, education, urban livelihoods, or any combination thereof.

Edith Stein was the student of Edmund Gustav Albrecht Husserl, who by most accounts established the field of phenomenology. Stein argues that empathy is enacted through reinforcing modalities of accomplishment. First, the experience of the Other emerges before the subject: "It faces me as an object (such as the sadness I 'read in another's face')."[29] Then, I put myself in the place of the Other by reproducing the form of their experience in my own imagination.

This, in turn, clarifies the Other's experience, which "faces" me again with added richness, contrasts, and contours as it takes on personalized, and personified, attributes. The process is not linear but iterative.

To Craig's question: I *did* see the laughing, smiling faces. The gestalt of that day was, well—I want to say it was infectious. But what does that mean? Well, it feels like what Stein postulated when trying to map out what it means to become empathetic. Those faces—the entire experience, really—pulled me in. Thoughts that day went to my own time as a ten-year-old, to my son and daughter, too, ages eight and twelve, respectively. Doing this brought me "closer," phenomenologically speaking, to them as subjects. I desired, then, to further close that distance. I wanted to ask them questions, about their desires, feelings . . . their lives. If they had been adults, I would have wanted to spend more time with them beyond the farm, to get to know them in a role other than "student."

I wasn't with Craig during those earlier encounters, so I cannot say what specifically caused him to "get it" when it came to overcoming prior urban prejudices. But on that day, I felt something that Craig was feeling, too. And if we both felt it, others might as well.

CHAPTER 7

Forest to Table

I STATED EARLY ON that this is not one of those "come to the table" books. My suspicion toward that label as a solution to today's ills are not unlike those directed at professionally facilitated events designed to have people talk out their differences. First, it is hard to get those spewing hate—those most in need of an empathy intervention—to participate in either event. But in addition, the very premise that breaking bread together is valuable requires people to stick around until the final course is served. I have been to enough dinners where religion, politics, race, or sexual orientation were brought up in such a way that it caused the early departure of a table-mate or two.

While the dinner tables highlighted in this chapter helped afford good old-fashioned conversation, dialogue is only part of its focus. What this chapter is really about is the whole experience, including quotidian encounters that have been banished from liberal deliberative theory, which includes the disarming nature of *physically* eating good food together.

The idea that spawned the experiments in this chapter came to me during one memorable interview in 2016, during a visit to the North Star State—Minnesota.

The pavement turned to gravel, so I knew the driveway was close. Over one more crest and there it was, leading to a large red barn with its colorful patterns of quilt squares. Though I had an appointment with the Smith brothers, the Smith sisters-in-law ended up stealing the show.

The farm was situated a little more than an hour north of the Twin Cities, in the heart of central Minnesota. Dairy farmers. I was there because of the farm's recently installed robotic milker; I've also been studying the impacts of agricultural automation on farm succession and rural labor markets.[1]

Parking in front of the milking parlor, I thought immediately that there had been a scheduling snafu. I first noticed the rifle with its still-unblemished maple stock reflecting the early morning sun. It was leaning against the lowered tailgate of a very blemished Ford pickup. November. Tree-stand season. Someone had been hunting whitetail deer.

Susan and Lynn came out from an adjacent machine shed. My reluctant interviewees. Their consent to participate was quickly followed with the qualifier, "The boys run the farm." This was followed with, "In a prior life we were city girls," stated in a manner that conveyed neither pride nor embarrassment, as if telling me the day of the month. Both had spent the first 20-plus years of their lives in Minneapolis.

One grabbed the rifle as the other made a hand gesture in the direction of the shed. Walking toward the building, I learned that Pat, Susan's husband, scored a 12-point buck the day before, a trophy deer by any estimation.

You can tell how comfortable someone is around guns by how they handle them. Novices tend to hold them pinkies out, as if handling a used tissue—a *heavily* used tissue, but you get my point. When Lynn grabbed the rifle, she reflexively pulled back the bolt to make sure the chamber was clear. It is the first thing taught to anyone handling a gun for the first time, at least when in the presence of a responsible adult.

I was right. While neither hunted, they both admitted to finding shooting "enjoyable." Neither, however, had fired a single shot prior to meeting the man they now wake up alongside every morning.

They offered to make coffee before answering the questions listed on the survey instrument in my backpack. The topic of hunting, and by extension guns, seemed as good as any to discuss at this point. They were comfortable talking about the subjects. As any journalist and social scientist can attest, establishing a good rapport with respondents is key to establishing trust. And besides, these two had an interesting story to tell.

"The conversion didn't happen overnight." Susan was trying to explain how she went from being "totally anti-gun," which is how she described herself upon first meeting Pat. It took a little unraveling to get at the catalyst of the conversation: food.

Lynn appeared with a pie. There was a refrigerator against the wall to my back, which is why I had not seen it. Without asking, she sliced me a piece the color of tar. "Grab yourself a plate and have a slice. How you taking your coffee? Black?"

Most know the dessert these days by its $20 name of flourless chocolate cake. In these parts, it goes by a less swanky title: mud pie. A plate on my lap and a cup of black coffee in my right hand, I listened to both explain their change of heart on arguably the most politically tribal subject of all: guns.

Lynn described her household growing up, noting that "almost everything we ate was local and organic." Her future husband, knowing this, played up these characteristics when describing the wild-game meat in his deep freeze. As Lynn spoke, Susan feverishly nodded her assent. "Same story here," she confirmed a few minutes later. "The meat demystified the guns, gave them a purpose," is how Lynn put it.

Even after they were married, Susan hated having guns in the house. Her courtship with Pat lasted less than a year. It took two hunting seasons before Susan "let up" on the subject and allowed her husband's firearms through the front door.

Both women were quick to note, however, that their respective households remained divided on the subject of political affiliation. The sisters-in-law remained registered Democrats, while the brothers maintained their lifelong Republican affiliation. But on the issue of guns, Lynn and Susan are at a different place from where they started.

Having returned the pie to the refrigerator, Lynn sank beside her sister-in-law on the futon. Both looked anticipant, the need to say something written on both faces.

Susan went first. "The gun owner: it's a stereotype for—."

"You can be pro–Second Amendment and not be a nut," Lynn cut it.

"Every gun owner we've met takes gun ownership seriously, as both a right and a responsibility," Susan explained.

Lynn again: "Like Susan was saying, it's pretty easy to demonize a caricature."

This back-and-forth competition with its rhythmic cadence happened whenever the subject was one that both were passionate about.

My conversation with Susan and Lynn was interesting. I am not trying to suggest anything more than that, to make it do anything more than to convey the point that it got me thinking. I also appreciate that Susan's and Lynn's experience, about only knowing gun owners who take ownership seriously, as both right and responsibility, isn't everyone's. I did not want to get into an argument with these two—remember, this was meant as an ice-breaker. Had this been part of the interview, I would have likely pushed them to clarify precisely what they meant by the comment. I know plenty of self-proclaimed responsible gun owners, for instance, who think that the St. Louis couple who, in 2020, pointed their guns at hundreds of racial injustice protesters marching on their private street were acting responsibly by doing that.[2] These are the same people who teach their children to never point a weapon, loaded or otherwise, at *anything* unless you intend to pull the trigger. Damn good advice. So, waving two guns at protesters doesn't sound very responsible to me . . . but I digress.

Susan and Lynn did eventually get to talking with their spouses about guns. But they were not goaded into these conversations. They came to them, rather, viscerally, nudged by, among other things, food. For Lynn and Susan, food helped to ground the gun debate, thus helping move the subject from out of the abstract shadows where culture wars are fought, to more concrete footing—not unlike what happened, perhaps, with the gay marriage debate in some households after so-called cultural warriors had loved ones disclose their previously hidden sexual orientation.

"He brought me venison sausage on our second date," Susan said of Pat. Lynn nodded and told me about the elk steaks she was regularly fed during her courtship with Jack. Food created an invitation to talk about a subject often off-limits, even among intimates. But more than that, it opened the door for other encounters, to which Lynn and Susan, over time, found themselves receptive. These experiences ranged from holding guns to standing in tree stands and helping field dress freshly harvested game.

If you think all gun owners, or, conversely, all gun control activists, are wackos, what facts could I possibly tell you to get you to engage with them openly and honestly on the subject?

I am reminded of when Donald Trump Jr. gave a lecture in an auditorium across the street from my house, about 100 yards from my front door. It was late October 2019. Judging by the protestors' chants, the US government's border incarceration and related child-separation policies were at the forefront of their minds. Gun control was mentioned too—it had been a horrific year for mass shootings.

One of the more popular chants, led by someone with a handheld loudspeaker, was, "*Donald Trump, lick my butthole!*"

We are well beyond thinking the conversations Susan and Lynn ultimately had with their husbands, premised on openness and honesty, can occur organically. Susan and Lynn even *loved* who they were speaking to, yet neither wanted to initially hear what their spouses had to say on the subject—remember Susan's early house ban. It took something visceral to get them there. It took food.

It's about More Than Guns

I grew up in a small town in northeastern Iowa. One of its residents was an avid hunter who, for a time, held irregularly scheduled wild-game dinner parties. I cannot recall everything served, though I do remember being introduced to snapper turtle soup. Everything offered was harvested by the host. Forest to table.

The *New Oxford English Dictionary* chose *locavore* as its 2007 Word of the Year. Farm-to-table dinner parties are replacing the bowling leagues, card parties, and church guilds that represented baby boomer conviviality. The wild-game dinners I remember attending as a child seem about as desirable to my urban, progressive foodie friends as camo fabric, high fructose corn syrup, and Rush Limbaugh merchandise. They want their protein to be free-range and organic but, what—*domesticated*?

There is an opportunity here.

Ted and I first met in 2007. He was erecting pea plant supports on his plot of ground at a community garden in Denver. I was getting a tour of the grounds with some of the garden's board of directors. The frequency of our encounters was minimal, until his youngest moved to California. He had considerably more free time on his hands after that.

He regularly volunteered the term *community organizer* when asked to self-describe his role in the community—his "real vocation," as he called it. (His paycheck came from Hewlett-Packard, for providing IT support, which he could do from his home.) Other terms that could also be used to describe Ted: lifelong Denver resident, African American, animal-welfare-friendly agriculture proponent, and progressive liberal. "Hillary's practically a Republican," he nearly shouted from a booth in a restaurant, as if wanting the world to know his politics, when describing his vote for Senator Sanders in the 2016 presidential primaries.

Ted's fondness for ethically raised, and I assumed ethically harvested, meat made him the perfect candidate for a wild-game dinner invite. I knew before asking that he would go. But it wasn't only his fondness for protein that gave me this confidence. Proceeds from the wild-game dinner I was inviting him to went to support the town's public library—Ted's deceased wife had taught literature to teenagers. He accepted the invitation, with suspicions. I doubt that he bought what I told him about the one-shot principle, that most hunters would rather come home empty-handed than inflict suffering on prey. Ethical harvest: only making kill shots. Yet he also admitted that the steak and hamburger in his deep freeze came from animals whose end was likely not far off from that experienced by a deer shot with a 180-grain bullet. Captive bolt gun: stun gun. Hunting rifle: gun gun. Pick your poison. The end result is the same.

Not all wild-game dinners are alike. Some follow the industrial livestock model. At those, death and all the undesirable elements of the animals' animality, for lack of a better term, are scrubbed clean from the event. Having attended a few, I have found their ultimate focus to be on the chef. Cast as modern-day alchemists, those preparing the food take something wild, something whose flesh is notoriously "gamy," and civilize it with a mix of heat and a few other ingredients that cause properties of the meat to change. The success of these events, then, often hinges on the audience's response to this performance, which in turn is a reflection on the cook's ability to make one forget they're eating *wild* game.

Alternatively, the wild-game dinner I invited Ted to, and those I grew up with, had a very different feel. At these events, one was not allowed to forget that the game consumed came from undomesticated territory.

The sun had long since set, enveloping the car in darkness. The county road we were driving along was unlit. Save for the distant glow of Denver on the horizon and the light from our headlights and dashboard, there was little illumination, which meant talking had to substitute for looking. With little to occupy our attention other than Desiigner playing in the background, Ted took it upon himself to reflect on what he had learned from the dinner.

"I'm no closer to calling myself pro-gun, 'cause I know what those things can do." Ted lost a cousin to gun violence when they were both teenagers. He added, reflecting on the dinner we had just left and the people met, "But I might have gotten a few things wrong. My image of what those guys believe might not be true. It has given me something to think about."

We both let the comment hang in the air. Before I had a chance to formulate a follow-up, Ted obliged: "I still don't like 'em—guns. But I have a new appreciation for why some do." After letting out a small chuckle, like what you might hear to convey disbelief, he added, "They act as if they can't live without 'em."

Earlier that evening, we had eaten a meal surrounded by hunters and gun owners. As Ted learned, you cannot talk about guns in a vacuum. Just as there are underlying reasons why ethanol policies are more salient for my corn-producing farmer friends in Iowa than for individuals like Ted, the subject of guns for Second Amendment supporters cannot be abstracted from who they are and what they believe in. In that sense, Ted's comment—*They act as if they can't live without 'em*—is perceptive.

To Ted's left at the dinner sat Nicole, an elementary-school teacher from the community. She knew the organizers of the event because they occasionally hunted with her husband. She labeled herself and her husband as "gun nuts." It's an American colloquialism used among gun enthusiasts to describe themselves. When directed *at* a gun enthusiast, however, it is typically meant as a put-down.

Back in the car, Ted reflected on what Nicole had told us. He exclaimed, "It's about guns, but it also isn't. Did you notice that?"

I could hear him draw in a deep breath. His response sounded more distant than before, as though he had turned his head from me and was talking to the window. I imagined him using the darkness much like a mathematician uses a blank chalkboard, for divining inspiration.

"To talk like, 'Our way of life is being regulated to death.'" He was repeating something Nicole had said to us. "Her concern wasn't about the Constitution, about being able to buy assault rifles. It was *existential*." Intonation made the last word pop in that small enclosed space.

Gun enthusiasts come in all colors, creeds, and religions and with different zip codes. Some US groups, however, are more likely to own a gun than others.[3] For example, 39 percent of men report personally owning a gun, compared to 22 percent of women. And while 36 percent of whites identify as gun owners, 24 percent of blacks and 15 percent of Hispanics make the same admission, even though one of the most pervasive images in our media culture is the armed black man (or boy). White men are especially likely to own a gun, at 48 percent, compared to white women and nonwhite men (24 percent each) and 16 percent of nonwhite women. Where people live also matters, with 46 percent of those living in rural areas reporting gun ownership, compared with 28 percent of those in the suburbs and 19 percent in urban areas. Moreover, three-quarters of those in rural areas claim to own more than one gun, compared with 48 percent of urban gun owners. "Protection" tops the list of reasons for owning for both groups, though gun owners in rural areas are far more likely than urban owners to also cite hunting, by almost a 2 to 1 margin.[4]

Returning to the scene in the car: Is this existential concern, to use Ted's stark terminology, justified?

What Ted was able to pick up on was a general unease felt by much of rural America, a worry—an existential one—that their values and way of life are being ridden roughshod over by a demographically superior urban population. You need only look at recent federal elections for evidence of this. Before 2016, it had been decades since rural residents voted *that* uniformly as a political block.

Part of me wants to add that this is especially a *white* rural American anxiety, as a lot of this restlessness involves white people seeing "their" ways of life changing. But having interviewed numerous rural Americans of color, who express similar sentiments about guns and who also talk of losing "their" rural culture, I cannot bring myself to reducing this unease to race alone. Rural studies scholars, including myself, have introduced the idea of talking about rurality as a performance, along the lines of how gender theorists like Judith Butler talk about gender, where neither are self-evident *things* as much as practices that people *do*.[5] Thinking in this way, then, allows us to root this rural anxiety in fears about losing heteronormative, hypermasculine expressions of rurality, of which gun culture—at least the type espoused by, say, the likes of the NRA—is certainly part.

For Nicole and others from that night, then, the gun debate is a proxy for something much bigger. For many at that dinner, it represents a struggle animated by a belief that what it means to be a rural American is being asymmetrically shaped by people who have not a clue about what this life is like, other than through stereotypes.

Ted also got to know Clarence, who gave an impassioned defense of gun rights that night. His defense of "keeping the government out of our gun safes" hinged on a profound, and not entirely unjustified, worry that rural livelihoods are being "legislated out of existence." A wheat farmer, Clarence was quick to equate government restrictions on the Second Amendment with other laws "choking out oil and gas industries—anything associated with rural economies is being put out of business." He was quick to add that his own livelihood, farming, was at risk of being choked out of existence, adding, "It feels like we're getting it from all angles." He never fully specified just what the "it" was he was getting from all sides. The closest he came to an explanation: "I want to say *the shaft* but that probably isn't specific enough for you. Okay, let's say what we're getting from all sides is being told what we can't do and how we ought to live by a bunch of people who don't give two shits about what happens to rural people."

Think about how calls to wean ourselves from coal or old-growth timber are often made without a shred of concern for communities and people dependent on those industries. The same can be said about most calls to end meat consumption, as if cattle live their entire lives in concentrated animal feeding operations. Never mind that those cattle all started somewhere, on cow-calf operations, also known as ranches, *family* ranches. I am not saying we should not think about transitioning toward renewable energy and away from practices that cannot be sustained well into the future. But if we are going to do that, then we need to think long and hard about what happens to those communities and the livelihoods dependent on unsustainable extractive practices. Knowing how little support in terms of public and private sector investments goes into these failing communities, it *does* look like no one gives "two shits" about whether the people there live or die.

Walking into the community hall, Ted and I were greeted immediately by a rifle pointed at an adjacent wall—a Winchester Model 70. The well-dressed man in a cowboy hat and lamb leather blazer next to the gun was selling raffle tickets. The rife was a door prize. Proceeds from the raffle ticket sale went to supporting the local library. In the back of the dining area was a demonstration tree stand. Elevated some six feet off the ground, it proved a popular destination for the event's preteen attendees.

This was not one of those events predicated on the erasure of history, where acts like hunting and field dressing, and the cultural symbols attached to those practices, are scrubbed. Unlike *those* dinners, where one's vision of a wild-game dish extends only as far as the kitchen but not beyond, this event was designed to be combined with images connecting forest and fork.

I mention this because the observation feels empirically important. Give me a little runway as I try sussing out this point.

The extended mind thesis by Andy Clark and David Chalmers launched an entirely new field called extended cognition.[6] This is the notion that our "minds" extend beyond the brain, even the body. This has been especially well-documented with Alzheimer sufferers who maintain a high level of functioning within a familiar space—like the home they've spent their lives in. These external props are arguably just as much part of these individuals' "cognitive machinery" as, say, their prefrontal cortex, to the point of scrambling a part of either produces disastrously similar effects.[7]

I am not suggesting that the rifle, tree stand, and décor of camo and wildlife decoys had become part of our minds that evening. They did, however, weigh on the conversation in the sense that they made it hard to have the safe, sanitized encounters that we might prefer in this hyperpartisan moment. Ted, for instance, used those props—wisely, in my opinion—as conversation starters. Not knowing the first thing about any of this stuff—he had never even *held* a gun—he asked questions. Pointing to the tree stand, he asked in a sincere tone, "What's that?" He repeated the question, in so many words, pointing to the rifle—a reference to the gun's model and caliber, not to the gun itself.

You could say the artifacts helped connect Ted to others around us that evening in a way that afforded opportunities for learning and, ultimately, understanding.

This case is as good as any, and better than most, to tease out elements of empathy to which I have yet to give proper attention—difference and alterity. These concepts speak not of recognition of sameness or even similarity, but rather of the appreciation, perhaps in some instances even awe, at a life and set of experiences that are wildly different from one's own. As argued by philosopher Emmanuel Levinas, developing a respect for alterity is as important to human relationships as recognizing commonality, such as through "our" shared humanity.[8]

The irony is not lost on me, talking about a black man acquiring an appreciation of difference toward white, rural lives that looked different from his own. I had not stated this explicitly. But, yes—that dinner was overwhelmingly populated by white people.

That difference was, in fact, precisely what stirred within Ted the aforementioned reflection and introspection toward this group during our car ride home, about past actions and attitudes and his own mental and emotional orientations, respectively. "It's like they're from another planet," he kept repeating. Not a response you'd expect to hear from someone about others with whom he is learning to empathize? How, after all, can you experience another's common humanity if you think them otherworldly? But that was not where Ted was coming from. This is where his aforementioned general benevolence is important. His comment was meant to signify that his various compasses, which had been his guide by telling him what *is* and *ought* to be, perhaps need to be reevaluated when applied to this group. This is what I took him to mean when he explained, "I can't claim to know what they feel if they're really coming from a place like that, where the right to bear arms, any arms, is viewed as an inalienable right. It was pretty clear they felt that way." He paused long enough to turn the radio off and silence the noise that tries to pass as playful radio banter these days. "I sure as hell don't feel the same, but I admit we're coming from different places."

In some ways, then, maybe Ted was primed for this journey. You might say, to play on the metaphor, that his bags were not only packed, but he had equipment already with him to hit the ground running—the equivalent of Google translate downloaded and all-weather clothes, actual experience doing multiculturalism, and so forth. Anyone who knows Ted would agree that he has a big heart. That description is particularly apropos here.

I have wondered what those white gun enthusiasts thought of Ted. They never talked about the color of his, or their, skin. If asked, I am sure none would have self-identified as a racist, a statement many would have likely attempted to prove by listing off their friends of color. I did not expect the topic of race to voluntarily come up, either. I do not want to speak for everyone there that night. But I did know some rather well. Those I knew all ticked the boxes of someone who is blinded by the ideology of colorblindness. They readily claimed to not see color. They did not believe in systematic racism, pointing to Obama's presidency as proof. This all matters because, to paraphrase the findings of a recent study out of the *American Journal of Community Psychology*, people who support colorblind ideology show less intergroup empathy and are less likely to act against prejudice.[9] Ted, alternatively, was not colorblind, which perhaps helps explain that capacity he appears to have shown for intergroup empathy.

Deep in the Heart . . . of Texas

The three of us were in a car—45 minutes from San Antonio, Texas, our destination—my two car-mates (graduate students I had employed to assist me with my research) and me.

From the back seat, "Have you ever seen a town this small. How'd you find this place?"

Then, from the front seat to my right, pointing to an old-fashioned hitching post in front of the town's post office, "Yeah, this is *wild*."

We were in the area to conduct interviews. But that was not what brought us to that particular town at that particular moment. We were there to eat.

"This is it," I said as the rented Chrysler 300 rolled to a stop a few yards from one of those portable signs with the cascading lights outlining an oversized arrow. The sign read, "Wild Game Dinner 2017."

Both student research assistants were accustomed to metropolitan landscapes, having spent all of their collective 45 years in one: back seat, Ben, Denver; passenger seat, Lukas, the California Bay Area. The saying *baptism by fire* entered my mind more than once as we approached the door to the festivities.

You could hear the enormity of the space before entering, the concentration of hundreds of simultaneous conversations. The room was as long and wide as a machine shed and almost as tall—a bustle of noise, punctuated with the odd shout and the chink of cutlery as volunteers hustled. Tables were arranged much like in a school cafeteria; lined one after another, five lines deep, they ran the length of the room, almost. At one end was a makeshift stage decorated with more than a dozen rifles and a giant barrel wrapped in chicken wire containing raffle tickets. That was the closest either had ever gotten to a firearm, other than those disabled for museum display purposes.

We eventually sat down to eat. Between bites of venison Parmesan, elk sausage, salad (cobb with shredded pheasant and wild boar bacon bits), pulled wild boar sandwiches, and rabbit stew (a.k.a. Hasenpfeffer), actual conversations had time to take shape.

Lukas was seated next to Jeff, a long-haul trucker a few years his senior. After Lukas declared his newfound love for venison Parmesan, never having had deer before, his seatmate volunteered to describe the contents of his garage chest freezer, which had "hundreds" of pounds of deer meat. He explained this as matter-of-factly as if he were describing the change in the front pockets of the Carhartt jeans he was wearing.

I took this as an invitation, and apparently Lukas did too. He asked, "Oh, you hunt?"

What started between Lukas and Jeff grew after only a few exchanges. It helped that Jeff had one of those voices—sharp like a Ring-necked Pheasant's claw. It was easy to pick out against the background noise. Soon those around us were talking, confirming what the three of us had suspected. We were surrounded by gun enthusiasts.

By meal's end, the entire corner of the table had contributed to the conversation. A lot of information was shared. If there was any doubt whether this was NRA country, it disappeared before I had finished my salad—which I ate first.

I am not going to talk about the more tribal bits of the conversation, debating the veracity of whether, say, Obama really does "hate freedom" and wants to "kill the Second Amendment." A lot was said—some tribal, some not.

One of those more open moments came as Jeff tried explaining his support for the Second Amendment. He first contextualized it historically, arguing that "the reason we won the Revolutionary War against the British military is the militia, because of private citizens taking up arms." He went on to explain how the Second Amendment exists as a check. He asked, "We have the military to protect us from invading forces but what do we do if government itself becomes corrupt?" The question elicited such strong head nods from around the table that it must have looked like they were headbanging to music only locals could hear.

I have heard this justification a lot over the years from gun owners. Self-described "gun nuts" might say they love guns. After some probing, however, what you will often find is that they love something else.

Those on the Left often view the Right's self-described adoration of "freedom" and "liberty" as at best empty signifiers—bumper sticker material but not much else. Or at worse, it is taken as hate masquerading as political philosophy, remembering Obama's analysis arguing that many on the Right "cling" to their guns and religion as a response to feeling bitter and anxious about the world.[10]

That is not how Jeff and others at the table saw their support for the Second Amendment. What they had described was actually rather practical, rather *American*; at least, that is how I would describe a desire to build into our political system as many checks as possible. Guns might not be the constitutional equivalent of the three branches of government, but for this group they are every bit as important to ensure against the rise of state-led tyranny as, for example, the press.

Those at the table were small-d democrats, which is to say, each supported the idea of democracy, the separation of powers among the branches of government, freedoms for everyone, and, most important, free and fair elections of the people and by the people. Of course, what these values ought to mean can and does vary widely. The phrase "of the people and by the people" can lead to support of the Electoral College or its abolishment, depending on your standpoint. Similarly, "freedoms for everyone" can still perpetuate racist attitudes and behaviors, as exemplified by colorblind ideology, where treating everyone the same perpetuates systemic racism.[11] Regarding those seated around that table, their support for the Second Amendment was rooted in a deep commitment to democracy, to the point of wanting super-processes in place in case electoral mechanisms become debased.[12]

But what does it mean, to go back to Jeff's quote, to view the Second Amendment as a check "if government itself becomes corrupt?" With COVID, we are seeing militias taking to the streets or, worse, responding to what some are calling overreach by state and local government officials. The FBI stopped a planned kidnapping and murder of Michigan's governor, Gretchen Whitmer, by arresting 13 militia members in October 2020.[13] One person's *corrupt* government is another's example of *responsible* government—look no further than the crimes that happened on January 6, 2021, and the discourses behind those actions, with the storming of the US Capitol. Doing something in the name of democracy does not entitle people to a free pass for their actions and beliefs. The country's founders were small-d democrats who managed to pervert their political philosophy just enough to justify slavery. Yet a democracy rooted in empathy, respect for difference, and care is not the same as one that exists through echo chambers and political tribes. I have a lot more confidence in small-d democrats when guided by the former as opposed to the latter.

Something very interesting happened that evening at the wild-game dinner. We talked about guns without getting into a debate over the value of guns. Are firearms good or bad? Do people kill or do guns? *Not* the questions we ought to be engaging in. Instead, because of the unique opportunity provided by the dinner and the empathy it afforded—a point I'll circle back to in a moment—the discussion was between people who learned that they held shared interests, like around protecting the safety of children and respecting cultural practices and identities.

My two progressive guests did not turn Republican that night. But they were moved by the experience.

Lukas and Ben processed what they had experienced moments earlier during our drive back to the hotel. Lukas confessed that prior to this night, he never had "any real conversation with a card-carrying member of the NRA." He had a sportscaster's precise way of speaking; every word spaced and dropped with the precision of a metronome. This made the stumbling and stammering in this voice at that moment especially notable.

"I had my biases—*have* my biases. Have I lumped gun owners into the same box? Stereotyped them, I'd say. Yeah, I did that."

Finding that ecumenical precision, he started sounding again like his old self when he turned to discussing the setting of that evening—not only the food but the smiling faces, the aromas, and the hunting motif.

"The whole event was so welcoming," Lukas confessed, adding, "I wasn't expecting that, to feel like I didn't have to have my guard up, which is how I entered the situation, like I was entering enemy territory."

I have emphasized what was said during that dinner because what was said was important. But why it was important—why it was impactful—had a lot to do with the space of the encounter. The medium mattered in this case, at least as much as the message.[14]

With bellies full, we saw the rustic black-cherry tarts come out on server carts. The planners apparently had a larger crowd than expected, either that or someone was mathematically challenged in the kitchen. Whatever the reason, they were short on desserts. We were located near the end of the table, the wrong end in this case. When the cart got to us, it looked like the pastry case at a café at the end of a busy day.

"We can share!" the grandmother of eight next to Ben announced with a gentle pat to his hand, which had been resting between them on the table. The idea was immediately supported by others, as words of assent were voiced all around. Someone from across the table got up and disappeared long enough to retrieve extra plates from the kitchen. The tarts were divvied up in halves and passed around.

It was not the only act that night to afford conviviality, trust, and respect among otherwise distant tribes. There were others, like when Lukas dropped his napkin and a burly, bearded fella in camo somehow squeezed beneath the table and retrieved it or when Ben's 70-something seatmate pulled pen and paper from her purse and wrote out the recipe for the rabbit stew, after announcing that it was her daughter who made it.

Any of these acts, by themselves, could easily be seen as downright quotidian. *He picked up a napkin? Big whoop.* But what was collectively done that night had everything to do with what was heard, which, as we know, matters just as much as what gets said.

Bringing the Heartland Home

My dog's wagging tail told me that the guests had started to arrive. It was late 2016, not long after interviewing Susan and Lynn Smith, the sisters-in-law introduced at this chapter's beginning. Meeting them gave me the idea for this meal and the motivation for taking people to wild-game dinners.[15]

The first to arrive were Jessica and Toby, friends of mine from Cheyenne, Wyoming. They operated a meat-processing business—effectively butchers, specializing in wild game, which in the Equality State meant they processed a lot of antelope, deer, elk, moose, and bear. (The state slogan comes from the fact that Wyoming was the first state to grant women the right to vote, in 1869, which, not coincidentally, also helped ensure that there would be enough voting citizens to meet the population requirement for statehood.) Jessica and Toby were also avid hunters, held strong NRA-type views about the Second Amendment, and were lifelong Republicans.

Next to arrive: Donald. The sound of his large diesel truck could be heard long before he pulled into my driveway. Donald was my other hunter-NRA-guest that evening, though since taking a job as an oilfield pumper, he has had no time to apply for an elk tag. If you are not familiar with the job, Donald assured me that it involves exactly what the title describes. "I make sure oilfield pumps *pump*."

The remaining invitees arrived before Donald could take off his steel-toed boots. Roze and Clark were active in northern Colorado's

local food scene. In addition to regularly volunteering at a food coop-
erative, they were fixtures at many of the area farmers' markets, believing strongly in the principle that as consumers we cast a vote every time
we make a purchase. And, last, Elena—a professor in the humanities
at Colorado State University. In her late twenties, she was new to the
Intermountain West, a recent transplant from Upstate New York.

It was a modern iteration of the odd couple, times three. Roze,
Clark, and Elena were lifelong Democrats—three never–gun owners
who had, at different times, likened NRA-members to terrorists. The
other three were diehard Republicans. Each had labeled Obama a
terrorist at least once in my presence.

The division of labor for the meal broke down as follows. I offered
unrestricted access to my house, including its alcohol cabinet and beer
fridge; Roze, Clark, and Elena brought the meal's salads and desserts;
and Jessica, Toby, and Donald supplied its mains: wild-game dishes. I
never cast the event to attendees as about bridging political divisions.
These were my friends, and I thought it would be fun getting them
together. That said, I am a curious guy.

If I could bring this group together, I recall thinking, *anything is
possible.*

This took place in 2016, a presidential election year, a year politics was on everyone's mind but not always on their tongues, at least
not among polite company when you suspected the person you were
talking to might be from the "other side." The initial conversation
was free-flowing but entirely safe, centering on things like biography
("Where are you from?") and jobs, which was when everyone learned
what an outfield pumper does.

The wild-game dishes on the menu for the evening—slow cooker
pulled venison and elk short ribs—came to my house prepared and
fully cooked. I just needed to get internal temps somewhere north of

130 degrees Fahrenheit. This was done easily enough. We were eating an hour after introductions.

I was the one who broached the subject. Knowing the ribs came from an animal taken some six months prior, I asked Donald to tell us about it. He obliged, in his own unique way. Donald is short and square, like the bed on his dually pickup truck. Every inch of him seems charged with an energy that can be sensed the moment he enters a room. And he is never negative or perfunctory about anything, which only adds to that electric glow.

"Oh, it was the peeerrrrrfect hunting trip. Zero wind. Slightly overcast. Mild."

When he got to the part of stalking the elk whose ribs lie before us, his top half—he was seated—broke into a type of performance art, moving his arms, hands, and head to accentuate the story. He spotted the animal at about 1,000 yards and crawled on his belly until the rangefinder registered he had cut the distance in half. At that point, he set the center of the reticle on the intended target and squeezed the Remington 700's trigger.

Elena asked him to explain the rationale for the 500-yard shot. If you think ethical hunting is an oxymoron, you have never heard someone like Donald talk about what he called the hunting ethic. He explained the one-shot principle, followed by a brief tutorial on Bullet Ballistics 101, where he talked about penetration and expansion—projectile properties that vary depending on the ammunition shot.

Comfortability around his newfound friends growing, he ended his lecture waxing eloquent. "The animals I eat died by my hand and in-front of my eyes and I thank them for this"—pointing to the meat and bones in front of us, then again to the ceiling above. He proceeded to then note what he described as hypocrisy among those who mistake hunters as "bloodthirsty savages," adding, "this coming from those who mindlessly live off animals, eating hamburgers and wearing leather, without wanting a drop of blood on their hands."

The discussion whirled in multiple directions after that. Without any shepherding on my part, the conversation remained centered on firearms, hunting, and the Second Amendment. These people wanted to talk about the subject, even though, or perhaps *because*, attendees were in the presence of others with a very different standpoint on the subject. Donald was the only one to out his tribal affiliations that evening, in a big away—"I bleed Republican." Yet enough had been said to make the political leanings of the others fairly transparent.

So: *why*? Why did these individuals choose to touch the political equivalent of the third rail by talking about guns with people not like themselves?

For one thing, the encounter afforded that evening consisted of familiar convivial acts: sharing of food and recipes—Elena brought a salad that everyone wanted to make at a later date; gestures of kindness, from fetching beers and refilling wine glasses to holding out chairs, taking coats, and laughing at Clark's dry sense of humor; and the passing of iPhones so we could have a look at each other's children. The space afforded *the opposite* of the elbows-out response you would have expected had my guests been invited under the pretense of talking about Second Amendment–type issues with those from the other side.

Even when the discussion "went there," the space helped diffuse participants' tribal instincts. I was especially struck by how having the wild game physically in front of us acted as a conduit that helped focus the discussion in an important way. Have you ever engaged with someone about guns who thinks differently on the subject than you? Ever notice how the conversation almost always immediately goes to grand debates that are, for all intents and purposes, irreconcilable? *Guns are great! No they're not!* The cooked flesh gave the conversation a welcomed level of, for want of a better term, concreteness. Our firmly planted forks helped anchor the discussion on everyday concerns that mattered for those around the table, like why Elena felt unsafe when encountering someone carrying a gun in public—Colorado is an open-carry state. Or, alternatively, Jessica shared she only felt safe when carrying a concealed weapon in her purse—the state also allows concealed carry, with a permit—though in light of Elena's admission, the firearm remained out of sight.

It is worth pondering if it also helped that there was a woman on the pro-gun side, especially knowing the links between so-called gun culture and hypermasculinity.[16] While Donald and Toby left no chances for misinterpretation when performing their masculinity, the off-colored joke by Donald about the size of his slugs typifying these displays, Jessica did not fit that mold. The ankle boots, well-manicured nails, Coach purse, and red lipstick would have made for an interesting juxtaposition had she pulled out that concealed handgun.

Jessica and Toby remained after the others left. They were spending the night. Cheyenne was far enough away that it would have been rude of me not to offer a spare bedroom. I offered a nightcap before showing my guests to their room. Toby was one of those who could drink black coffee, and usually did, immediately before going to bed. Jessica and I sat opposite him at my kitchen table. We both took in the rich aroma from Toby's mug, wishing we could partake.

Jessica spoke first, in a voice that harbored neither sarcasm nor malice: "I think it's safe to say that I just had dinner with people who I don't usually eat with"—they had met Donald before, so it was clear who she was talking about.

Toby followed, as if to make sure I understood that their comments came from a place of appreciation. "We enjoyed their company. I just hope they enjoyed ours. Like Jessica says, we're coming at issues from different places, our politics and such."

We proceeded to talk about those "different places," with the help of some nudging on my part. Heartfelt information had been shared—made possible by specific practices and situational realities highlighted earlier—and I was especially interested in hearing if any of that information had gotten through.

Jessica gave the strongest indication that it had.

"If I knew all gun-control advocates were like those three, I'd be inclined to be open to arguments in support of things like Red Flag Laws and universal background checks."

Jessica could not intuit the political stances taken by Roze, Clark, and Elena during their short time together. As I said, discussion remained polite throughout—politics was only discussed tangentially. Jessica's comments were animated by the fact that she encountered her left-leaning dinner mates as fellow humans rather than enemies. This was allowed because the situation encouraged a receptiveness—*allowed* is as good a term as any, realizing these six would have shut down in most other situations when confronted by this otherness.

Toby summed up the arc of the experience best. "The whole thing about the gun laws snuck up on me," he explained, adding, "I was like, 'Weren't we just talking about food?' Then it was about guns. But it was cool—I didn't feel the least bit defensive talking about it."

Here's to the promotion of encounters that substitute elbows-out defensiveness with good food, friendship, and heartful encounters.

CHAPTER 8

Final Thoughts and New Trajectories

I WOULD LIKE TO SPEND a little time unpacking what I mean by today's incivility problem, realizing that a hate-fueled mass shooting is not commensurable with, say, targeting a politician at a restaurant with vulgarity and insults. Incivility hurts feelings; it might even frighten. It does not, however, liquify bodily organs or orphan (or kill) children. But remember also, civility can be highly unempathetic.

So: what am I arguing against? Hate? Incivility? Both? It's complicated. Civility and incivility, in certain contexts, can facilitate empathy. This raises another question: what can I say about empathy after having spent more than a decade looking for it? Let's first look at the concept of (in)civility, before coming around one last time to empathy.

Norbert Elias's brilliant tome *The Civilizing Process*, first published in the 1930s, ripped the veneer off of civility discourse: parading as discernment, while masking, regardless of intention, the effects of power and other forms of oppression in the name of preserving the status quo. The same can be said of speech deriding bad manners or that evoking such derogatory labels as *uncouth*, *boorish*, and *impolite*. As John Doris writes in *Lack of Character*, the "discourse of character often plays against a background of social stratification and elitism."[1]

I am not arguing against civility. A wholesale rejection of aspirations to be more civil throws the baby out with the bathwater. Yet I worry that that is precisely what we are doing by disparaging those who are said to be showing too much emotion in their politics. *Sit down, behave, and talk it out!* Did I not just spend an entire book criticizing solutions that show a little too much enthusiasm for that (small-l) liberal worldview?

I also want to be careful suggesting anger as a suitable foundation for empathy—though, thanks to Martha Nussbaum's *Anger and Forgiveness*, I realize now that there are different species of emotion. Talking through anger's role in all of this, and how some of those emotions might be leveraged to engender empathy, might prove useful as we contemplate next steps.

Anger, according to Nussbaum, is a response to create an illusion of control where we feel none. She frequently talks about anger in the context of grief and intimate betrayal, often in the context of spousal infidelity. But betrayal, of course, takes many forms. I have heard people talk about feeling betrayed by, for instance, one's government, politicians, Wall Street, and the police. And you can bet the sense of harm felt in many of those instances cuts every bit as deep as adultery. The Black Lives Matter Movement—there's an example of what intense betrayal can animate.

Nussbaum suggests, when confronting an injustice, a need for practicing forward-looking action, whereas anger is always backward-looking; the past, she reminds us, cannot be changed. Anger, in fact, can only exacerbate the very grievances and tensions that brought about the emotional responses in the first place: "It makes one think that progress will have been made if the betrayer suffers, when, in reality, this does nothing to solve the real problem. It eats up the personality and makes the person quite unpleasant to be with. It impedes useful introspection. It becomes its own project, displacing or forestalling other useful projects. And importantly, it almost always makes the relationship with the other person worse."[2]

Sound familiar?

Instead of anger, Nussbaum introduces what she calls "transition-anger" as a positive way to respond to harms against us or those dear to us.[3] Called a species of anger, it has little resemblance to it since it lacks the desire for harm. The content of transition-anger is something akin to shouting from one's window, *I'm mad as hell and I'm not going to take it anymore!* but without the intent of committing harm. The emotional response is entirely forward-looking—not about retribution but about the search for justice through nonviolent cooperation.

She notes, too, that it isn't just people who need to change. Our political system as a whole is not only unjust but premised on elements of vengeance, retribution, and violence, to say nothing about the deeply intertwined relationships between masculinity and violence. Yet she also rightly realizes that if we want anything to change, it is *us* who are going to have to make it happen. As James Baldwin once told Margaret Mead during a public exchange in 1970, "We've got to be as clear-headed about human beings as possible, because we are still each other's only hope."[4]

I avoided talking about this earlier without the proper framing: the *suffering* afforded some respondents through the experiences described in prior chapters. But rather than feeling harmed, they expressed gratefulness for the pain. Of course, the question that then needs to be asked is, What have they *done* with that disposition?

I mention this because it speaks to Nussbaum's argument in the terms of where she eventually lands on the subject of guilt, which she defines as anger at oneself. Though confessing to having once believed guilt had value, Nussbaum now sees it as irrational and unproductive. But her rejection of guilt is based on a false premise: that guilt can only be felt as self-directed violence—a type of penitence, whereby through pain one is redeemed.

Lydia participated in the berry experiment. At the beginning of the study, she proudly declared to have "no sympathy for Mexican immigrants," later adding, "They choose to be here; they can also choose to go back if they don't like it."

Lydia's time picking was largely uneventful. She spent her time plugging away by herself, without saying much to anyone. Even during lunch, she sat crisscross on the ground a good 10 feet from anyone else. Her silence masked what must have been a robust internal dialogue.

"The work: it sucked," she deadpanned when asked to comment on the picking experience one week later. After a beat she added, for clarification, "I mean, I'm grateful for the experience. It just stirred up some stuff, caused me regret."

A pregnant pause ensued. Lydia wanted to take me somewhere, but it felt like she needed to lead me there, without my prodding. I was worried I might scare her away from an important admission if I pushed.

"I regret the coldhearted stuff I've said about these people for trying to make a living and feed their kids." During a moment of particular honesty, she admitted feeling "especially bad" about what she said in front of her two teenagers. This "stuff" included derogatory language about Spanish-speaking immigrant populations.

I also noticed a redirection indicated by Lydia's frustration. Transition-anger, perhaps? The individualized resentment (e.g., scapegoating) I had detected in earlier interviews had turned into anger at broader institutional inequities. As Lydia quipped in our final interview, "Americans aren't losing jobs to immigrants so much as to globalization," adding, "Why beat up on a group that's every bit as screwed as the rest of us."

I am frustrated with globalization, too. And I am trying to work through my own anger toward those free-market globalizers who cannot seem to grasp the harm of what they worship, having gotten to know many through my research: executives from some of the world's largest food companies; venture capitalists making seven-plus-figure investments into agriculture's so-called digital revolution; and individuals from such neoliberal organizations as the World Bank, the US Federal Reserve, and the International Monetary Fund. As I tell the left-leaning activist friends of mine who hold individualized resentments, a few have even burned in effigy individuals whom I've interviewed—I have met the enemy, many times over, and they turned out to be . . . well, *human*. It is hard to hate someone once you learn that, for many of them at least, their motivations reside in also wanting to leave the world better off than when they came into it.

Misdirected anger and indiscriminate suffering *are* wildly problematic. But those phenomena are different from anguish that arises out of sharing in some of a survivor's pain after realizing your contribution to it.

As someone promoting the heartland, it would be hypocritical of me to reject the place for passion in politics and civil engagements. But I also agree completely with the critique that civility discourse has been a tool historically to squelch difference. On the one hand, the term *incivility* speaks to all the negative ideologies that have come up throughout this book—racism, xenophobia, elitism, classism. We should be civil if that means rejecting those "isms." On the other hand, incivility, emotion, and passion need to disrupt the close-mindedness that gets hidden behind rhetoric of believing our opinions are 100 percent right. There is no way we can get by peacefully if we blind ourselves to other worldviews.

Hope Springs Eternal . . . but I Tend toward Wanting a Strategy

While I have talked about it a lot, this isn't really a book about food. The real protagonists are the *encounters*, which touch us viscerally

and have leveling abilities, built on leveraging our collective enthusiasm toward food. Are there examples of this that extend beyond
food systems?

Whatever the solution, we cannot rest on the hope that a
100-flowers-blossoming approach—a more poetic way of saying,
let's start throwing stuff out and see what sticks—is going to pull
us through. Who does not know about the virtues of empathy? Its
value is enshrined in every major world religion, though you can be
forgiven for forgetting that, given how some of the converted treat
others. Barbara Ehrenreich's masterful *Nickel and Dimed* has sold a
gazillion copies since its release in 2001.[5] Yet our empathy for the poor
remains lacking, especially if they look or speak differently from those
with whom we regularly associate.

Strong leadership backing effective policy has been the engine of
much of America's transformative change. We need a hate-eradicating
moonshot, something that provides direction, encouragement, and
support. We need leaders who can visualize changes to food policy
and civic engagement and articulate strategies for seeing those ideas
through to implementation. We need to think big by . . . wait for it:
going S-M-A-L-L. Only through the quotidian and mundane can we
hope to circumvent those filters tuned toward defending against the
full-frontal attack.

Educational policy shifts from pre-K and up offer one obvious
place to start. The spell once cast by the headland approach on higher
education has already weakened considerably, as evidenced by the
rise of experiential learning, community-based research, and flipped
classrooms, though professors still spend a lot of time professing.
Those who can't do, teach. Not true—we need to teach through doing.

Earlier, I discussed how certain groups, through, for instance,
geographic sorting, inhabit very different social spaces. Never the
twain shall meet. Schools, perhaps especially institutions of higher

education—I'm looking at *you* Land Grant universities—could leverage town-gown connections in ways that nurture empathy among otherwise disparate groups.

Classrooms, at all levels, have so-called sister classrooms, located in other locales. Usually these municipalities are in some faraway land, perhaps in the community's ancestral country. A neighboring town near where I grew up has a long and rich historical connection to what is now the Czech Republic. During the summer of 1893, the community was even home to the famed Czech composer Antonin Dvorak. I remember friends from this town learning about Czech culture, food, and a bit of the language. I love the idea of developing global competencies from a young age. But why stop there? Why not also select a community closer to home? Or even within one's own state? Picture it: a metropolitan school pairing up with another in a rural school district. Assignments could include learning about their "sibling"—the school, its community, people, and cultures, the area's history and industries. Perhaps students could FaceTime or Zoom with community and business leaders, elders, children—thanks to COVID, we're all used to these platforms now. The school year might end with a field trip to the community. Maybe some type of student-exchange program could also be established, a practice sure to afford encounters that engender empathy and dispense with caricatures.

Look at the curriculum at most institutions of higher education, animated by a well-intentioned desire to "create global citizens"—boilerplate language baked into most universities' strategic plans. Nothing wrong with that, as long as we are making sure to avoid producing adults who know nothing about people and communities closer to home. Speaking of my own students, most possess some level of important firsthand knowledge of international cultures, through practices made available to them thanks to study-abroad programs and an internationalized curriculum where visiting speakers from around the world give testament to their experiences. Yet there remain too many who have never set foot in a frontier country or who think broadband internet access is only a problem in other countries. Heck, I had a senior professor recently admit to me how, other than Colorado, and *metropolitan* Colorado at that, he has only spent time in the urban coasts, east and west, of the US.

To address this experiential gap, my own university—and I can proudly say that I am helping oversee this project, thanks to collaborations between Colorado State University (CSU) Extension and a handful of CSU colleges—began offering internship opportunities a few years back to connect students with communities around the state. CSU faculty and CSU Extension agents act as the students' mentors, as the latter are embedded in a community over the summer to help local residents address an issue of their choosing. The communities, in these instances, identify a research question they need assistance addressing. The students, meanwhile, work with community members to address those questions while acquiring personal experience conducting community-based field research. For some of my headstrong colleagues, they see this as a way to train students for a life in the academy. For me, it represents an example of just the type of heartland experience the academy ought to be providing the next generation.

These examples are not exactly moonshot caliber, and they speak largely to what we colloquially call the rural-urban divide. How about resurrecting Civilian Conservation Corps but this time directing it at food? The Civilian Conservation Corps, better known as simply CCC, was a voluntary public work relief program that operated from 1933 to 1942 in the US. It was part of President Franklin D. Roosevelt's New Deal, directed at providing manual labor jobs related to the conservation and development of natural resources in lands owned by federal, state, and local governments. A total of 3 million men participated in the CCC, which also provided them with shelter, clothing, and food.[6]

The CCC was only directed at men—hugely problematic, enough said—and the un- and underemployed. While a model to consider, it cannot be treated as a cookie cutter. It would have to be significantly reworked to address issues we are grappling with today.

Speaking of public service: let's talk more about public service. Early in 2019, a federal panel released its report on whether the US ought to require its citizens to perform public service, as many other countries do. (The report was released in the middle of a government shutdown, adding both irony and seriousness to the subject.) To quote Joe Heck, chairman of the National Commission on Military, National, and Public Service: "In a country of more than 329 million people, the extraordinary potential for service is largely untapped." While reluctant to provide a full-throated endorsement of mandatory public service, the commission voiced support of figuring out how to "create a universal expectation of service" in which every American is "inspired to and eager to serve."[7]

In the wake of COVID, this might be exactly what we need. Think about it, an *actual* CARES Act—an epistemic and empathetically oriented stimulus package designed to engender an ethic of care that matches in scope the Coronavirus Aid, Relief, and Economic Security Act. After months of being told by public health professionals and governments to avoid others, at least within a six-feet radius, I can think of no better way to celebrate the defeat of the virus than to have the pendulum swing in the other direction. We are likely going to need it.

If we do not actively work to once again be comfortable around people, I fear more will be lost to COVID than hundreds of thousands of lives. I've been able to empirically document this point with research conducted since the outbreak: that all this social distancing has taken its toll, causing some to grow fearful of public encounters—to say nothing about how it has impacted people differently depending on their race, class, and gender.[8] The virus has also been used to deepen distrust of already-othered groups, like Asians or Latinx: the former, blamed for causing the pandemic; the latter, likened to super spreaders.[9]

This all matters not just because it's wrong to demonize others, whether for political gain or otherwise. We also know fear negatively impacts how we think about and interact with those whom we hold anxiety toward. For example, when individuals with liberal orientations were exposed to a physical threat during a study, their political and social attitudes instantly, though temporarily, became more conservative. This explains why some pundits and politicians choose to exploit fear for political gain. They are manipulating very deep, some say biologically rooted, motivations to avoid threatening uncertainties.[10] One study, conducted during an H1N1 flu epidemic, involved reminding participants of the dangers of the flu virus and then asked them their attitudes toward immigration, after which they were queried whether they had been vaccinated against flu yet.[11] Those who hadn't received their flu vaccination were more likely to be anti-immigration than the ones who felt less threatened. In a follow-up study, participants were offered hand sanitizer immediately after the flu warning and the immigration bias went away. Elsewhere, researchers asked individuals to imagine themselves as completely invulnerable to any harm—as superheroes.[12] Everyone's attitudes toward issues like immigration became less hostile as they no longer felt a need to scapegoat immigrants for harms to which they were now impervious.

In short, the longer we continue fearing having experiences with others—to say nothing of the long-term impacts of attributing CO-VID-19 to certain groups, like by calling it the "China virus"—the harder it will be to journey collectively to the heartland. I am not suggesting that social distancing has no purpose. Keeping six feet apart might be *physical* distancing but we should not kid ourselves in thinking it is only that. By the time this book sees the light of day, I can only hope we are at a different place, where we can talk in terms of "after COVID." In *that* world, I bet there are going to be certain COVID-related habits we will have to intentionally unlearn.

A nugget of wisdom frequently attributed to Warren Buffett, which he is said to have passed along more than once to Berkshire Hathaway investors, is this: "You only find out who is swimming naked when the tide goes out." Mr. Buffett first made the comment in 1992, after Hurricane Andrew exposed inequities in the insurance industry, to describe how systemic recklessness and dangers cannot be easily hidden during times of chaos and crisis.[13] I have heard this quote a lot lately. The tide, thanks to COVID-19, has gone out in a big way. It is more than the emperor who is without clothes.

Talking is not enough to make people see eye to eye, not when some think they have an obligation to keep others safe by wearing a mask while others cry foul, seeing mask-wearers as infringing upon their right to develop herd immunity—I actually had someone tell me that. The risks associated with COVID, the value of masks, the price of social distancing: those are yet other examples of debates that cannot be settled by facts alone. Again, and again, and again . . . our world is rocked by crises that require more heartfelt encounters. We need an empathetic revolution.

Giving in to Empathy

Empathy, much like civility, has a complex past. The concept's modern political roots are often traced back to the work of Scottish philosophers Adam Smith and David Hume.[14] Following this tradition, empathy is frequently understood as a technique through which "we" can come to know the cultural "other." So to empathize is often taken to mean having the "capacity to gain a grasp of the content of other people's minds, and to predict and explain what they will think, feel, and do."[15]

As a qualitative and inductively inclined social scientist (which is simply to say, one who tries to follow the data whenever possible), it made me uncomfortable saying too much early on about what I think empathy is. I wanted to bring you along on these journeys, first, to let you experience some of what I experienced before elaborating on where I landed on the topic. After having witnessed others confronting otherness to the extent detailed in prior chapters, I have some discomfort deploying such a positivist understanding of empathy as spelled out in the prior paragraph.

Empathy should not be about emotional equivalence, let alone about predicting the thoughts, feelings, and behaviors of others. Is there a way, then, to afford experiences that are less about enabling (privileged) subjects to take the role of the other and more about nurturing affective perspective-taking that is diffused, multiple, and contested? If *that* is empathy, then it becomes less about putting one self in another's shoes and more about experiencing multiple positionalities, including from the standpoint of how one's own positionality perpetuates damaging practices rooted in neocolonial and neoliberal relations. Not everyone discussed in prior chapters reached this understanding. But some did.

This helps give space for what Carolyn Pedwell calls alternative empathies, which refers to those attunements that seek to *give up* on mastering another's standpoint while "*giving in* to being affected by that which is experienced as 'foreign' in the midst of transnational flows, relations and power structures."[16] Empathy is at its most productive, from this perspective, when the aim ceases to be about reaching a shared understanding, which only ends up erasing the very differences in need of embracing—remember what I said earlier about the dangers of colorblind ideology. Empathy, or empathies, if you prefer, ought to exist because of contradictions and antagonisms, not in spite of them. I witnessed this productive dissonance countless times in the field and after. This is what happens when subjects are made to rethink the positionality of others by also reflecting on their own norms and conventions and coming to a place that recognizes difference as productive and not something to be feared.

The 2020 Presidential Election: What Now?

The 2020 presidential election is now behind us. Years prior, when I was beginning to write this book, people whom I consider far smarter than I advised me not to make this book about any one person. Whether after four years or eight, Trump will eventually not be president. Best to look forward.

Yet, given what has just happened, I can't *not* end things without talking about the 2020 presidential election and all that happened after . . . and that continues to happen. (It is May 2021, and the Arizona GOP is conducting an "audit" of votes cast in Maricopa County; some still think that election was rigged. *Oy vey!*) And maybe we shouldn't put that election behind us. Just under 47 percent of the votes cast—more than 74 million US adults—picked Trump. Over the last four years, I was able to explain, and thus explain away, his 2016 win. "I voted for him but didn't actually think he'd *win!*" I cannot tell you how many times I heard that. Or: "I really thought he'd behave and do the right thing, act presidential, once he became president." That excuse was told to me more than any other, in so many words. I know others have heard these rationalizations, too, which is why the 2020 election was such a gut punch for so many. Disgust now substitutes for what had been disbelief. We can all think of a time of working through feelings of incredulity toward someone or something. Loathing, however, is a whole different ball game when the aim is reconciliation. It is hard to agree with calls to "put differences aside" when so many are just plain *wrong* about so much—science, institutional racism, white privilege, COVID, the importance of a free press, the 2020 election . . .

While trying to be balanced and engage in a big tent–type of strategy, I want to call out and repudiate "bothsidesism."[17] This is when things that are not the same are made to appear the same, thus allowing bad actors to pass off disinformation as fact—like when someone (i.e., Trump) says there are "very fine people on both sides" when talking about white supremacists.[18] In this environment, the goal for the latter is not about winning an argument but about having their nonsense taken seriously.

There is only one side when it comes to demonstrating grace and compassion for those whose basic rights are not being valued. Black lives do matter. Science shouldn't be denied, nor should it be ignored. No human is "illegal." Now, of course, if someone doesn't believe any of that, there is nothing I can say to make them think otherwise. That's why a book like this is so important. As I have noted again and again, we need to start by thinking in terms of heartland experiences. Save headland confrontations for those times when they'll actually work, after heads have been primed by the heart. That same refrain is also what I would say to Never Trumpers. I do hold out hope for reconciliation. But first, hearts will need changing.

Getting there will require abandoning those naive "coming together" tropes that perpetuate bothsidesism and that assume today's violent acts of incivility are based on matters of differing opinions. With so many steadfast in their belief that they are "on the right side of history," and just plain right in their convictions, it is foolish to think any meaningful encounters can be had where the expressed purpose is acknowledging "we" are wrong while admitting the truth claims of "others." This also explains my fascination with food. It can both motivate and disarm, creating a potential entry point to understanding without participants even knowing it.

For those appalled by the outcome of the 2020 presidential election—and yes, I realize this references people across the political spectrum—I am not proposing that you change your convictions. If you have it in you to imagine a world in which we do see each other empathetically and feel like you can move in that direction, then do it, but be prepared to be surprised at where you end up, because empathy itself isn't always as it first appears. And for those who can't see themselves from any other standpoint, that's okay, too. You just have to eat.

Acknowledgments

To my wife, Nora Carolan, my deepest thanks for more than a decade of unimaginable support and love. Thank you to my mom and dad, Clair and Faye Carolan, for always being there and for teaching me about food growing, harvesting, canning, freezing, pickling, cooking, smoking, baking, and eating. As for our children, Elena and Joey— well, thanks for giving me a reason for wanting to remake the world in a way that affords compassion and empathy. And of course, this book could not have been written were it not for the hundreds who populate its pages. To those who participated in my research over the years, my sincerest appreciation to you all.

For reading and meticulously commenting on the manuscript, I thank Sue Ring deRosset. To my editor at Stanford University Press, Marcela Cristina Maxfield, thank you for your enthusiastic determination in helping me get these stories told. Thanks, too, to the anonymous reviewers. Your support at the front and back ends of this process meant more than you know. I am also grateful to Stanford University Press for publishing my words and giving me this opportunity to share my journey and to Colorado State University for allowing me space to do what I love.

Notes

Chapter 1. Journeys to the Heartland

1. Carolan, M. 2017. *No one eats alone: Food as a social enterprise.* Washington, DC: Island Press.

2. All names of interviewees are pseudonyms to protect the identity of respondents and to ensure, as promised, their anonymity.

3. See, e.g., Sturgis, P., and Allum, N. 2004. Science in society: Re-evaluating the deficit model of public attitudes. *Public Understanding of Science, 13*(1), 55–74.

4. Hillary Clinton famously branded Trump supporters with this title. See Holan, A. 2016. In context: Hillary Clinton and the "basket of deplorables." PolitiFact. www.politifact.com/article/2016/sep/11/context-hillary-clinton-basket-deplorables.

5. See, e.g., Howe, P. D. 2018. Perceptions of seasonal weather are linked to beliefs about global climate change: Evidence from Norway. *Climatic Change, 148,* 467–480; Stern, P. C., Kalof, L., Dietz, T., and Guagnano, G. A. 1995. Values, beliefs, and proenvironmental action: Attitude formation toward emergent attitude objects. *Journal of Applied Social Psychology, 25*(18), 1611–1636.

6. See, e.g., Habermas, J. 1998. *Between facts and norms: Contributions to a discourse theory of law and democracy.* Cambridge, MA: MIT Press.

7. Lodge, M., and Taber, C. 2013. *The rationalizing voter.* New York: Cambridge University Press.

8. Mason, L. 2018. Here's how political science explains the GOP's obsession with civility. *Washington Post,* June 28. www.washingtonpost.com/news/posteverything/wp/2018/06/28/heres-how-political-science-explains-the-gops-obsession-with-civility/?noredirect=on&utm_term=.72ec7921828b.

9. See, e.g., Van Bavel, J. J., Baicker, K., Boggio, P. S., Capraro, V., Cichocka, A., Cikara, M., Crockett, M. J., Crum, A. J., Douglas, K. M., Druckman, J. N.,

and Drury, J. 2020. Using social and behavioural science to support COVID-19 pandemic response. *Nature Human Behaviour, 4*, 460–471.

10. Novelly, T. 2018. Crowd cheers when valedictorian quotes Trump. Then reveals it was Obama, *USA Today*, June 3. www.usatoday.com/story/news/politics/2018/06/03/kentucky-valedictorian-quotes-trump-then-reveals-obama/667758002.

11. See, e.g., Brosend, W. 2018. *Preaching truth in the age of alternative facts.* Nashville, TN: Abingdon.

12. Bolsen, T., Druckman, J. N., and Cook, F. L. 2015. Citizens', scientists', and policy advisors' beliefs about global warming. *ANNALS of the American Academy of Political and Social Science, 658*(1), 271–295, 271.

13. Chua, A. 2018. *Political tribes: Group instinct and the fate of nations.* New York: Penguin; Kornacki, S. 2018. *The red and the blue: The 1990s and the birth of political tribalism.* New York: Ecco.

14. Langton, L., and Masucci, M. 2017. Hate crime victimization, 2004–2015. Bureau of Justice Statistics, June 29. www.bjs.gov/index.cfm?ty=pbdetail&iid=5967.

15. Carolan, M. 2017. More-than-active food citizens: A longitudinal and comparative study of alternative and conventional eaters. *Rural Sociology, 82*(2), 197–225.

16. Enos, R. 2017. *The space between us: Social geography and politics.* New York: Cambridge University Press.

17. McCarthy, J. 2017. U.S. support for gay marriage edges to new high. Gallup, May 15. http://news.gallup.com/poll/210566/support-gay-marriage-edges-new-high.aspx.

18. Pew Research Center. 2016. Religion and public life, Sept 28. www.pewforum.org/2016/09/28/5-vast-majority-of-americans-know-someone-who-is-gay-fewer-know-someone-who-is-transgender.

19. See, e.g., Buckley, M. 2017. Notable Christians who've had a change of heart on LGBT issues. Religion News Service, July 12. https://religionnews.com/2017/07/12/notable-christians-whove-had-a-change-of-heart-on-lgbt-issues.

20. Florida, R. 2017. How place shapes our politics. Bloomberg CityLab, Dec. 12. www.citylab.com/life/2017/12/how-place-shapes-our-politics/548147; Reny, T. T., Collingwood, L., and Valenzuela, A. A. 2019. Vote switching in the 2016 election: How racial and immigration attitudes, not economics, explain shifts in white voting. *Public Opinion Quarterly, 83*(1), 91–113; see also Wetts, R., and Willer, R. 2019. Who is called by the dog whistle? Experimental evidence that racial resentment and political ideology condition responses to racially encoded messages. *Socius, 5*, 1–20, https://journals.sagepub.com/doi/

pdf/10.1177/2378023119866268.

21. Stacey, M., Carbone-López, K., and Rosenfeld, R. 2011. Demographic change and ethnically motivated crime: The impact of immigration on anti-Hispanic hate crime in the United States. *Journal of Contemporary Criminal Justice, 27*(3), 278–298.

22. See, e.g., Albarracin, D., and Shavitt, S. 2018. Attitudes and attitude change. *Annual Review of Psychology, 69*, 299–327; Wolsko, C., Ariceaga, H., and Seiden, J. 2016. Red, white, and blue enough to be green: Effects of moral framing on climate change attitudes and conservation behaviors. *Journal of Experimental Social Psychology, 65*, 7–19.

23. Wolsko, Ariceaga, and Seiden. Red, white, and blue enough, 10.

24. Wolsko, Ariceaga, and Seiden, 10.

25. Kahan, D. M. 2013. Ideology, motivated reasoning, and cognitive reflection. *Judgment and Decision Making, 8*(4), 407–424. http://journal.sjdm.org/13/13313/jdm13313.pdf.

26. Carpenter, D. 2017. Button making. Heritage Crafts Association. http://heritagecrafts.org.uk/button-making.

27. *Telegraph* Reporters. 2012. Where do milk, eggs and bacon come from? One in three youths don't know, *The Telegraph*, June 14. www.telegraph.co.uk/foodanddrink/foodanddrinknews/9330894/Where-do-milk-eggs-and-bacon-come-from-One-in-three-youths-dont-know.html.

28. U.S. Farmers and Ranchers Alliance. 2011. Nationwide surveys reveal disconnect between Americans and their food. Cision PR Newswire, Sept. 22. www.prnewswire.com/news-releases/nationwide-surveys-reveal-disconnect-between-americans-and-their-food-130336143.html.

29. Linkage Research and Consulting. n.d. Growing consumer interest in food production. https://linkageresearch.com/consumer-food-production.

30. International Food Information Council Foundation. 2019. 2018 food and health survey. https://foodinsight.org/wp-content/uploads/2018/05/2018-FHS-Report-FINAL.pdf.

31. Schermer, M. 2015. From "Food from nowhere" to "Food from here": Changing producer-consumer relations in Austria. *Agriculture and Human Values, 32*(1), 121–132; Campbell, H. 2009. Breaking new ground in food regime theory: Corporate environmentalism, ecological feedbacks and the 'food from somewhere' regime? *Agriculture and Human Values, 26*(4), 309–319.

32. Lempert, P. 2014. Almost all shoppers watching cooking shows. *Supermarket Guru*, Nov 5. www.supermarketguru.com/articles/almost-all-shoppers-watch-cooking-shows.

33. Hunter. 2020. Food study 2020: Special report, America gets cooking.

Hunter Public Relations, New York/London, April 9. www.slideshare.net/ HUNTERNY/hunter-food-study-special-report-america-gets-cooking-231713331.

34. Carolan, M. 2021. COVID-19's impact on gendered household food practices: Eating and feeding as expressions of competencies, moralities, and mobilities. *Sociological Quarterly.* https://doi.org/10.1080/00380253.2020.1870415.

35. French, S. A., Tangney, C. C., Crane, M. M., Wang, Y., and Appelhans, B. M. 2019. Nutrition quality of food purchases varies by household income: The SHoPPER study. *BMC Public Health, 19*(1), https://doi.org/10.1186/s12889-019-6546-2; Darmon, N., and Drewnowski, A. 2015. Contribution of food prices and diet cost to socioeconomic disparities in diet quality and health: A systematic review and analysis. *Nutrition reviews, 73*(10), 643–660.

36. Gray, B., and Kish-Gephart, J. 2013. Encountering social class differences at work: How "class work" perpetuates inequality. *Academy of Management Review, 38*(4), 670–699; Kraus, M., Piff, P., Mendoza-Denton, R., Rheinschmidt, M., and Keltner, D. 2012. Social class, solipsism, and contextualism: How the rich are different from the poor. *Psychological Review, 119,* 546–572.

37. See, e.g., Kerner, S., Chou, C., and Warmind, M. 2015. *Commensality: From everyday food to feast.* London: Bloomsbury; Waters, A. 2008. *Slow Food Nation's come to the table: The slow food way of living.* New York: Modern Times; Carolan, M. 2017. *No one eats alone: Food as a social enterprise.* Washington, DC: Island Press.

38. Bowen, S., Brenton, J., and Elliott, S. 2019. *Pressure cooker: Why home cooking won't solve our problems and what we can do about it.* New York: Oxford University Press.

39. See, e.g., Cairns, K., and Johnston, J. 2018. On (not) knowing where your food comes from: Meat, mothering and ethical eating. *Agriculture and Human Values, 35*(3), 569–580; Cairns, K., Johnston, J., and MacKendrick, N. 2013. Feeding the "organic child": Mothering through ethical consumption. *Journal of Consumer Culture, 13*(2), 97–118; Knaak, S. J. 2010. Contextualising risk, constructing choice: Breastfeeding and good mothering in risk society. *Health, Risk & Society, 12*(4), 345–355.

40. Fielding-Singh, P. 2017. A taste of inequality: Food's symbolic value across the socioeconomic spectrum. *Sociological Science, 4*(17), 424–448, 424.

41. See, e.g., Lubrano, A. 2018. Attacking people in poverty for buying birthday cakes and other treats with food stamps, *Philadelphia Enquirer,* June 18. www.inquirer.com/philly/news/food-stamps-lobsters-birthday-cakes-snap-poverty-20180617.html.

42. Shandwick, W., Tate, P., and KRC Research. 2018. *Civility in America 2018: Civility at work and in our public squares.* www.webershandwick.com/wp-content/uploads/2018/06/Civility-in-America-VII-FINAL.pdf.

43. Bonn, T. 2020. Overwhelming majority of voters say civility is needed in politics. *The Hill*, Feb. 3. https://thehill.com/hilltv/rising/481217-overwhelming-majority-of-voters-say-civility-is-needed-in-politics.

44. American Psychological Association. 2018. *Stress in America: Generation Z*. Survey, Oct. www.apa.org/news/press/releases/stress/2018/stress-gen-z.pdf.

45. One of the reviewers used this turn of phrase, which I liked and adopted.

46. Bornstein, D. 2018. Recovering the (lost) art of civility. *New York Times*, Oct. 29. www.nytimes.com/2018/10/29/opinion/recovering-the-lost-art-of-civility.html; Peru, A. 2018. Initiative for public deliberation teaches civil facilitation and dialogue skills. *Clark County Today*, Feb. 8. www.clarkcountytoday.com/news/initiative-for-public-deliberation-teaches-civil-facilitation-and-dialogue-skills/#.W_Xq4pNKg_U.

47. See, e.g., Mutual of Omaha. 2015. Donna and Bob—An unlikely friendship. www.youtube.com/watch?v=4dMMCVfKP9s&feature=youtu.be.

48. Jones, C. 2019. Report on the uncivil, hate and bias incidents on campus survey. The Lead Fund, Case Western Reserve University. www.aaaed.org/images/aaaed/LEAD_Fund/LEAD-Fund-Report-UHBIOC-Report.pdf.

49. Grigonis, H. 2017. Cyberbullying happens more often on Instagram, a new survey suggests. *Digital Trends*, July 20. www.digitaltrends.com/social-media/cyberbullying-statistics-2017-ditch-the-label.

50. Davis, T. 2019. Iowa teacher who posted "sniper rifle" comment about climate activist's visit resigns. *Des Moines Register*, Oct. 11. www.desmoinesregister.com/story/news/2019/10/11/greta-thunberg-iowa-waterloo-teacher-resigns-matt-baish-wcsd-police-sniper-rifle-comment-climate/3946175002.

51. Setty, G., Silverman, H., and Jackson, A. 2020. Man charged in death of 80-year-old after mask dispute in upstate New York bar. *CNN*, Oct 6. www.cnn.com/2020/10/06/us/new-york-mask-bar-death-trnd/index.html.

52. Ehrenreich, B. 2001. *Nickel and dimed: On (not) getting by in America*. New York: Holt.

53. I am deeply grateful to an anonymous reviewer who generously pointed me to the settlement house movement as a previous example of a successful journey to the heartland.

54. See Dewey, J. 1958. *Experience and nature*. New York: Courier Corporation; James, W. 1948. *Essays in pragmatism*. New York: Simon and Schuster; Peirce, C. 1934. *Pragmatism and pragmaticism*. Reprinted in C. Hartshorne and P. Weiss (Eds.), *Collected papers of Charles Sanders Peirce* (vol. 5). Cambridge, MA: Harvard University Press, 1974.

55. Addams, J. 1896. *A modern King Lear*. Reprinted in J. B. Elshtain (Ed.), *The Jane Addams Reader* (pp. 163–176). New York: Basic Books, 2002; Addams, J. 1902.

Democracy and social ethics. Reprint, Urbana: University of Illinois Press, 2002.

56. I thank one of the anonymous reviewers for reminding me of this point. See also Lasch-Quinn, E. (1993). *Black neighbors: Race and the limits of reform in the American settlement house movement, 1890–1945*. Chapel Hill: University of North Carolina Press; and Yan, M. C. 2004. Bridging the fragmented community: Revitalizing settlement houses in the global era. *Journal of Community Practice*, 12(1–2), 51–69.

57. See, e.g., Glaser, J. M., and Berry, J. M. 2018. Compromising positions: Why Republican partisans are more rigid than Democrats. *Political Science Quarterly*, 133(1), 99–125; Morris, I., and Gervais, B. 2018. *Reactionary Republicanism: How the Tea Party in the House paved the way for Trump's victory*. New York: Oxford University Press.

58. Grossman, M., and Hopkins, D. 2016. *Asymmetric politics: Ideological Republicans and group interest Democrats*. New York: Oxford University Press.

59. Mason, L. 2018. Here's how political science explains the GOP's obsession (see note 8 above).

60. Keller, J. 2019. Republicans are the main purveyors of identity politics. *Pacific Standard*, March 1. https://psmag.com/social-justice/republicans-are-the-main-purveyors-of-identity-politics.

61. See, e.g., Bauerlein, M. 2012. Liberals, conservatives, and the Haidt results. *Chronicle of Higher Education*, April 23. www.chronicle.com/blogs/brainstorm/liberals-conservatives-and-the-haidt-results/46113; and Saletan, W. 2012. Why won't they listen? "The Righteous Mind," by Jonathan Haidt. *New York Times*, March 23. www.nytimes.com/2012/03/25/books/review/the-righteous-mind-by-jonathan-haidt.html.

62. Wetts, R., and Willer, R. 2019. Who is called by the dog whistle? Experimental evidence that racial resentment and political ideology condition responses to racially encoded messages. *Socius, 5*, 17. https://journals.sagepub.com/doi/pdf/10.1177/2378023119866268.

63. Carolan, M. 2020. "They say they don't see color, but maybe they should!" Authoritarian populism and colorblind liberal political culture. *Journal of Peasant Studies*, 47(7), 1445–1469. https://doi.org/10.1080/03066150.2020.1739654.

64. See Wise, T. 2010. *Colorblind: The rise of post-racial politics and the retreat from racial equity*. San Francisco: City Lights.

65. Judd, D., and Phillip, A. 2018. Pete Buttigieg says he understands the concern over past remarks on minorities and education. *CNN*, Nov. 26. www.cnn.com/2019/11/26/politics/pete-buttigieg-minorities-education/index.html.

66. Signorile, M. 2018. "Fuck Civility." *HuffPost*, June 27. www.huffpost.com/entry/opinion-signorile-civility-trump_n_5b31ad0de4b0b5e692f0c7b8.

67. Obama (in)famously remarked back in 2008 that many white working-class Americans were "bitter" and said they "cling to guns or religion." He also warned the Democratic establishment of what we now call Trumpism if the party continued to ignore certain working-class segments of the electorate. See, e.g., Spross, J. 2016. How Obama diagnosed Trumpism way back in 2008. *The Week*, March 8. https://theweek.com/articles/610945/how-obama-diagnosed-trumpism-way-back-2008.

68. Davidson, H. 2020. Around 20% of global population under coronavirus lockdown. *The Guardian*, March 24. www.theguardian.com/world/2020/mar/24/nearly-20-of-global-population-under-coronavirus-lockdown.

69. Boxell, L., Conway, J., Gentzkow, M., Thaler, N. M., and Yang, D. 2020. Polarization and public health: Partisan differences in social distancing during the coronavirus pandemic. White paper. Cambridge, MA: Harvard University. https://sites.google.com/site/leviboxell/paper_storage/social-distancing.pdf; Lipsitz, K., and Pop-Eleches, G. 2020. The partisan divide in social distancing (May 7). Available at SSRN: https://ssrn.com/abstract=3595695 or http://dx.doi.org/10.2139/ssrn.3595695.

70. Pepinsky, T. 2020. Yes, wearing a mask is partisan now. https://tompepinsky.com/2020/05/13/yes-wearing-a-mask-is-partisan-now.

71. Williams, D. 2020. Target employee breaks arm in fight with shoppers who wouldn't wear masks, police say. *CNN.com*, May 12. www.cnn.com/2020/05/12/us/coronavirus-california-target-mask-assault-trnd/index.html.

72. Beauchamp, Z. 2020. The partisan culture war over masks. *Vox*, May 13. www.vox.com/2020/5/13/21257181/coronavirus-masks-trump-republicans-culture-war; North, A. 2020. What Trump's refusal to wear a mask says about masculinity in America. *Vox*, May 12. www.vox.com/2020/5/12/21252476/masks-for-coronavirus-trump-pence-honeywell-covid-19.

73. Burton, N. 2020. Why Asians in masks should not be the "face" of the coronavirus. *Vox*, March 6. www.vox.com/identities/2020/3/6/21166625/coronavirus-photos-racism.

74. Vazquez, M., and Klein, B. 2020. Trump again defends use of the term "China virus." *CNN.com*, March 19, www.cnn.com/2020/03/17/politics/trump-china-coronavirus/index.html.

Chapter 2. How Would You Stomach That?

1. This is a play on a phrase often attributed to Mark Twain. See, e.g., https://quoteinvestigator.com/2015/07/15/truth-stranger.

2. Thanks to rising tuition and runaway student debt, these two positions are not as far apart as they might at first appear.

3. See, e.g., Collins, P. H. 1986. Learning from the outsider within: The sociological significance of Black feminist thought. *Social Problems,* 33(6), s14–s32; and Hekman, S. 1997. Truth and method: Feminist standpoint theory revisited. *Signs: Journal of Women in Culture and Society,* 22(2), 341–365.

4. Williams, J. 2018. A prominent member of Germany's far-right anti-Islam party just converted to Islam. *Vox,* Jan. 24. www.vox.com/2018/1/24/16927978/germany-far-right-party-afd-islam-convert-arthur-wagner.

5. See, e.g., Feldmann, L. 2013. Coming out: How Sen. Rob Portman's gay son charted his path. *Christian Science Monitor,* March 25. www.csmonitor.com/USA/Politics/DC-Decoder/2013/0325/Coming-out-How-Sen.-Rob-Portman-s-gay-son-charted-his-path.

6. USDA Food and Nutrition Service. 2018. A short history of SNAP. www.fns.usda.gov/snap/short-history-snap.

7. Quoted in Philpott, T. 2019. Would the latest SNAP cuts kick a bunch of rich folks off food stamps? *Mother Jones,* July 23. www.motherjones.com/food/2019/07/would-the-latest-snap-cuts-kick-a-bunch-of-rich-folks-off-food-stamps.

8. Drawn from Olen, H. 2019. Billionaires and millionaires against food stamps. *Washington Post,* July 24. www.washingtonpost.com/opinions/2019/07/24/billionaires-millionaires-against-food-stamps.

9. RentCafé. 2020. Fort Collins, CO rental market trends. www.rentcafe.com/average-rent-market-trends/us/co/fort-collins.

10. See USDA Food and Nutrition Service. 2021. SNAP eligibility. www.fns.usda.gov/snap/recipient/eligibility.

11. Magness, J. 2018. Woman on welfare couldn't afford groceries. Cashier didn't let others help pay, witness says. *Miami Herald,* May 29. www.miamiherald.com/news/nation-world/national/article212096239.html.

12. Center on Budget and Policy Priorities. 2021. A quick guide to SNAP eligibility and benefits. Sept. 1. www.cbpp.org/research/food-assistance/a-quick-guide-to-snap-eligibility-and-benefits.

13. The Front Range, the north-south corridor anchored by Denver in the center, holds approximately 85 percent (4.9 million) of the state's total population (5.7 million).

14. Emch, M., Dowling Root, E., and Carre, M. 2017. *Health and medical geography.* 4th ed. New York: Guilford Press, p. 300.

15. See, e.g., Henning-Smith, C., Evenson, A., Kozhimannil, K., and Moscovice, I. 2018. Geographic variation in transportation concerns and adaptations to travel-limiting health conditions in the United States. *Journal of Transport & Health,* 8, 137–145; Holben, D. H., McClincy, M. C., Holcomb Jr., J. P., Dean, K. L., and Walker, C. E. 2004. Food security status of households in Appalachian Ohio with

children in Head Start. *Journal of the American Dietetic Association, 104*(2), 238–241.

16. Treuhaft, S., and Karpyn, A. 2010. The grocery gap: Who has access to healthy food and why it matters. PolicyLink/Food Trust. http://thefoodtrust.org/uploads/media_items/grocerygap.original.pdf.

17. Shergold, I., and Parkhurst, G. 2010. Operationalising "sustainable mobility": The case of transport policy for older citizens in rural areas. *Journal of Transport Geography, 18*(2), 336–339.

18. Giesel, F., Köhler, K., and Nowossadeck, E. 2013. Old and immobile in rural areas? Limited mobility of the elderly in the context of increasingly problematic health care in rural regions. *Bundesgesundheitsblatt, Gesundheitsforschung, Gesundheitsschutz, 56*(10), 1418–1424; Schwarzlose, A. A. I., Mjelde, J. W., Dudensing, R. M., Jin, Y., Cherrington, L. K., and Chen, J. 2014. Willingness to pay for public transportation options for improving the quality of life of the rural elderly. *Transportation Research Part A: Policy and Practice, 61*, 1–14.

19. See, e.g., Curry, S. J., Wagner, E. H., and Grothaus, L. C. 1991. Evaluation of intrinsic and extrinsic motivation interventions with a self-help smoking cessation program. *Journal of Consulting and Clinical Psychology, 59*(2), 318–324; Matson, D. M., Lee, J. W., and Hopp, J. W. 1998. The impact of including incentives and competition in a workplace smoking cessation program on quit rates. *American Journal of Health Promotion, 13*(2), 105–111.

20. See, e.g., Gomel, M., Oldenburg, B., Simpson, J. M., and Owen, N. 1993. Work-site cardiovascular risk reduction: A randomized trial of health risk assessment, education, counseling, and incentives. *American Journal of Public Health, 83*(9), 1231–1238.

21. See, e.g., Wing, R. R., Jeffery, R. W., Pronk, N., and Hellerstedt, W. L. 1996. Effects of a personal trainer and financial incentives on exercise adherence in overweight women in a behavioral weight loss program. *Obesity Research, 4*(5), 457–462.

22. Gneezy, U., Meier, S., and Rey-Biel, P. 2011. When and why incentives (don't) work to modify behavior. *Journal of Economic Perspectives, 25*(4), 191–210; Kamenica, E. 2012. Behavioral economics and psychology of incentives. *Annual Review of Economics, 4*(13), 427–452.

23. Close to 40 percent of voters in the state declare allegiance to no party.

24. Massumi, B. 2002. *Parables for the virtual: Movement, affect, sensation.* Durham, NC: Duke University Press.

Chapter 3. We're Being Pulled Apart

1. See Serra, N., and Stiglitz, J. E. 2008. *The Washington Consensus reconsidered: Towards a new global governance.* New York: Oxford University Press.

2. See, e.g., Ballard-Rosa, C., Jensen, A., and Scheve, K. 2018. Economic decline, social identity, and authoritarian values in the United States. Boston: American Political Science Association.

3. Ballard-Rosa, Jensen, and Scheve; see also Laurence, J., and Bentley, L. 2015. Does ethnic diversity have a negative effect on attitudes towards the community? A longitudinal analysis of the causal claims within the ethnic diversity and social cohesion debate. *European Sociological Review, 32*(1), 54–67; Recchi, E. 2015. *Mobile Europe: The theory and practices of free movement in the EU*. Basingstoke: Palgrave Macmillan.

4. See, e.g., Laurence and Bentley (note 3 above); and Van Heerden, S., and Ruedin, D. 2017. How attitudes towards immigrants are shaped by residential context: The role of ethnic diversity dynamics and immigrant visibility. *Urban Studies*, Oct. 25. https://doi.org/10.1177/0042098017732692.

5. Hendricks, G., Hanlon, S., and Madowitz, M. 2019. Trump's corporate tax cut is not trickling down. Center for American Progress, Sept 26. www.americanprogress.org/issues/economy/news/2019/09/26/475083/trumps-corporate-tax-cut-not-trickling; Blair, H. 2019. It's not trickling down, Economic Policy Institution, July 29. www.epi.org/blog/its-not-trickling-down-new-data-provides-no-evidence-that-the-tcja-is-working-as-its-proponents-claimed-it-would.

6. Bloch, S. 2020. President Trump described meatpackers' "liability problems." Here's what that could mean for workers. *The Counter*, May 7. https://thecounter.org/trump-meatpackers-liability-protection-tort-reform-tyson-covid-19.

7. Kindy, K. 2020. More than 200 meat plant workers in the U.S. have died of COVID-19. Federal regulators just issued two modest fines. *Washington Post*, Sept 13. www.washingtonpost.com/national/osha-covid-meat-plant-fines/2020/09/13/1dca3e14-f395-11ea-bc45-e5d48ab44b9f_story.html.

8. I refer here to the civil unrest in the town of Kenosha, which began in August 2020, following the police shooting of Jacob Blake, who was shot four times in the back during an arrest. The sentence also alludes to 17-year-old Kyle Rittenhouse, who drove up from Illinois and ended up shooting three protestors.

9. Tam Cho, W. K., Gimpel, J. G., and Hui, I. S. 2013. Voter migration and the geographic sorting of the American electorate. *Annals of the Association of American Geographers, 103*(4), 856–870; Martin, G. J., and Webster, S. W. 2020. Does residential sorting explain geographic polarization? *Political Science Research and Methods, 8*(2), 215–231 (originally published online Oct. 22, 2018); Nall, C. 2015. The political consequences of spatial policies: How interstate highways facilitated geographic polarization. *Journal of Politics, 77*(2), 394–406.

10. Kandel, D. B. 1978. Homophily, selection, and socialization in adolescent friendships. *American Journal of Sociology, 84*(2), 427–436; McPherson, J. M., and

Smith-Lovin, L. 1987. Homophily in voluntary organizations: Status distance and the composition of face-to-face groups. *American Sociological Review, 52*(3), 370–379.

11. Gimpel, J. G., and Hui, I. S. 2015. Seeking politically compatible neighbors? The role of neighborhood partisan composition in residential sorting. *Political Geography, 48,* 130–142; Gimpel, J. G., and Hui, I. 2017. Inadvertent and intentional partisan residential sorting. *Annals of Regional Science, 58*(3), 441–468.

12. See, e.g., Martin, G. J., and Webster, S. W. 2020. Does residential sorting explain geographic polarization? *Political Science Research and Methods, 8*(2), 215–231 (originally published online Oct. 22, 2018).

13. Huber, G. A., and Malhotra, N. 2017. Political homophily in social relationships: Evidence from online dating behavior. *Journal of Politics, 79*(1), 269–283.

14. Dvir-Gvirsman, S. 2017. Media audience homophily: Partisan websites, audience identity and polarization processes. *New Media & Society, 19*(7), 1072–1091, 1072.

15. Iyengar, S., and Krupenkin, M. 2018. Partisanship as social identity; Implications for the study of party polarization. *The Forum, 16*(1), 23–45.

16. Arceneaux, K., Johnson, M., and Cryderman, J. 2013. Communication, persuasion, and the conditioning value of selective exposure: Like minds may unite and divide but they mostly tune out. *Political Communication, 30*(2), 213–231.

17. Huckfeldt, R., Mendez, J. M., and Osborn, T. 2004. Disagreement, ambivalence, and engagement: The political consequences of heterogeneous networks. *Political Psychology, 25*(1), 65–95.

18. Huckfeldt, Mendez, and Osborn. Disagreement, ambivalence, and engagement, 91.

19. See, e.g., Gąsiorowska, A., and Hełka, A. 2012. Psychological consequences of money and money attitudes in dictator game. *Polish Psychological Bulletin, 43*(1), 20–26; Gino, F., and Pierce, L. 2009. The abundance effect: Unethical behavior in the presence of wealth. *Organizational Behavior and Human Decision Processes, 109*(2), 142–155; Kouchaki, M., Smith-Crowe, K., Brief, A. P., and Sousa, C. 2013. Seeing green: Mere exposure to money triggers a business decision frame and unethical outcomes. *Organizational Behavior and Human Decision Processes, 121*(1), 53–61; Piff, P., Stancato, D., Côté, S., Mendoza-Denton, R., and Keltner, D. 2012. Higher social class predicts increased unethical behavior. *Proceedings of the National Academy of Sciences, 109*(11), 4086–4091.

20. Vohs, K. D., Mead, N. N., and Goode, M. R.. 2006. The psychological consequences of money. *Science, 314*(5802), 1154–1156. doi:10.1126/science.1132491.

21. Vohs, Mead, and Goode, 1156.

22. Piff, Stancato, Côté, Mendoza-Denton, and Keltner. Higher social class predicts increased unethical behavior (see note 19 above).

23. Grewal, D. 2012. How wealth reduces compassion: As riches grow, empathy for others seems to decline, *Scientific American*, April 10. www.scientificamerican.com/article/how-wealth-reduces-compassion.

24. See, e.g., Besley, T. 2013. What's the good of the market? An essay on Michael Sandel's *What money can't buy. Journal of Economic Literature, 51*(2), 478–95; Sandel, M. 2012. *What money can't buy: The moral limits of markets.* New York: Farrar, Straus and Giroux.

25. Marwell, G., and Ames, R. 1981. Economists free ride, does anyone else? Experiments on the provision of public goods, IV. *Journal of Public Economics, 15*(3): 295–310.

26. See Carter, J., and Irons, M. 1991. Are economists different, and if so, why? *Journal of Economic Perspectives, 5*(2): 171–177.

27. Frank, R., Gilovich, T., and Regan, D. 1993. Does studying economics inhibit cooperation? *Journal of Economic Perspectives, 7*(2), 159–171; Frank, R., Gilovich, T., and Regan, D. 1996. Do economists make bad citizens? *Journal of Economic Perspectives, 10*(1), 187–192; Lanteri, A. 2008. (Why) do selfish people self-select in economics? *Erasmus Journal for Philosophy and Economics, 1*(1), 1–23.

28. For a review of this literature, see Sandel, *What money can't buy.*

29. Gneezy, U., and Rustichini, A. 2000. A fine is a price. *Journal of Legal Studies, 29*(1), 1–17.

30. Carolan, M. 2018. *The food sharing revolution: How start-ups, pop-ups, and co-ops are changing the way we eat.* Washington, DC: Island Press.

31. Peterson, A. 2016. Meet the site that is like Uber—but for tractors. *Washington Post*, May 6. www.washingtonpost.com/news/the-switch/wp/2016/05/06/meet-the-site-that-is-like-uber-but-for-tractors; see also, Zuckerman, J. 2016. Machinery Link: Where Uber meets agriculture, *North Virginian Daily*, June 23. www.nvdaily.com/news/2016/06/hold-machinery-link-solutions-where-uber-meets-agriculture.

32. Berry, J. M., and Sobieraj, S. 2013. *The outrage industry: Political opinion media and the new incivility.* New York: Oxford University Press.

33. USDA. 2017. In 2016, 73 percent of USDA school lunches were free or reduced price. www.ers.usda.gov/data-products/chart-gallery/gallery/chart-detail/?chartId=85337.

34. Berry and Sobieraj, *The outrage industry*, 82.

35. Media Matters staff. 2019. These are Sean Hannity's leading advertisers. *Media Matters*, July 26. www.mediamatters.org/sean-hannity/these-are-sean-hannitys-leading-advertisers.

36. Sanders, B. 2017. How corporate media threatens our democracy. *In These Times*, Jan. 26. http://inthesetimes.com/features/bernie-sanders-corporate-media-threatens-our-democracy.html.

37. Bort, R. 2018. This is what a pro-Trump local news monopoly would look like. *Rolling Stone*, June 25. www.rollingstone.com/politics/politics-news/this-is-what-a-pro-trump-local-news-monopoly-would-look-like-666068.

38. Clifford, C. 2018. Bernie Sanders: America is "owned and controlled by a small number of multi-billionaires." *CNBC.com*, Dec 12. www.cnbc.com/2018/12/12/bernie-sanders-america-is-controlled-by-a-few-multi-billionaires.html.

39. Noam, E. M. (Ed.). 2016. *Who owns the world's media? Media concentration and ownership around the world*. New York: Oxford University Press.

40. Wong, J. C. 2019. 8chan: the far-right website linked to the rise in hate crimes. *The Guardian*, August 4. www.theguardian.com/technology/2019/aug/04/mass-shootings-el-paso-texas-dayton-ohio-8chan-far-right-website.

41. Mandhana, N., and Haggin, P. 2019. New Zealand massacre video clings to the internet's dark corners. *Wall Street Journal*, March 17. www.wsj.com/articles/new-zealand-massacre-video-clings-to-the-internets-dark-corners-11552766810.

42. L, B. 2019. Deep dot web seized: The king is dead, long live decentralized markets? Terbium Labs, July 11. https://terbiumlabs.com/2019/07/11/the-king-is-dead-long-live-decentralized-markets.html.

43. Iqbal, M. 2020. YouTube revenue and usage statistics (2020). August 8. *Business of Apps*. www.businessofapps.com/data/youtube-statistics.

Chapter 4. Farming Familiarity

1. See Carolan, M. 2017. More-than-active food citizens: A longitudinal and comparative study of alternative and conventional eaters. *Rural Sociology, 82*(2), 197–225.

2. See, e.g., Ackerman-Leist, P. 2013. *Rebuilding the foodshed: How to create local, sustainable, and secure food systems*. White River Junction, VT: Chelsea Green; Obach, B., and Tobin, K. 2014. Civic agriculture and community engagement. *Agriculture and Human Values, 31*(2), 307–322; Pole, A., and Gray, M. 2013. Farming alone? What's up with the "C" in community supported agriculture? *Agriculture and Human Values, 30*, 85–100; Renting, H., Schermer, M., and Rossi, A. 2012. Building food democracy: Exploring civic food networks and newly emerging forms of food citizenship. *International Journal of Sociology of Agriculture and Food, 19*(3), 289–307.

3. National Agricultural Library. n.d. Community supported agriculture. US Department of Agriculture, Washington, DC. www.nal.usda.gov/afsic/community-supported-agriculture.

4. See, e.g., Farnsworth, R. L., Thompson, S. R., Drury, K. A., and Warner, R. E. 1996. Community supported agriculture: Filling a niche market. *Journal of Food Distribution Research*, 27(856-2016-56416), 90–98.

5. National Agricultural Library. n.d. Community supported agriculture. US Department of Agriculture, Washington, DC. www.nal.usda.gov/afsic/community-supported-agriculture.

6. Chen, W. 2013. Perceived value in community supported agriculture (CSA): A preliminary conceptualization, measurement, and nomological validity. *British Food Journal*, 115(10), 1428–1453.

7. United States Census. 2019. Quick Facts. www.census.gov/quickfacts/fact/table/CO,US/RHI125219.

8. Florida, R. 2017. The United Cities of America. *City Lab*, April 25. www.citylab.com/equity/2017/04/the-united-cities-of-america/520221.

9. United States Census. 2019. Quick Facts. www.census.gov/quickfacts/fact/table/fortcollinscitycolorado/AGE775217.

10. Johnston, J., Szabo, M., and Rodney, A. 2011. Good food, good people: Understanding the cultural repertoire of ethical eating. *Journal of Consumer Culture*, 11(3), 293–318; Hwang, J. 2016. Organic food as self-presentation: The role of psychological motivation in older consumers' purchase intention of organic food. *Journal of Retailing and Consumer Services*, 28, 281–287.

11. See, e.g., Cairns, K., Johnston, J., and MacKendrick, N. 2013. Feeding the "organic child": Mothering through ethical consumption. *Journal of Consumer Culture*, 13(2), 97–118.

12. Guthman, J. 2003. Fast food/organic food: Reflexive tastes and the making of "yuppie chow." *Social & Cultural Geography*, 4(1), 45–58; Shi, Y., Cheng, C., Lei, P., Wen, T., and Merrifield, C. 2011. Safe food, green food, good food: Chinese community supported agriculture and the rising middle class. *International Journal of Agricultural Sustainability*, 9(4), 551–558.

13. The actual quote reads, "Race doesn't really exist for you because it has never been a barrier. Black folks don't have that choice." Ngozi Adichie, C. 2013. *Americanah* (p. 23). New York: Alfred A. Knopf.

14. See, e.g., Laurence, J., and Bentley, L. 2015. Does ethnic diversity have a negative effect on attitudes towards the community? A longitudinal analysis of the causal claims within the ethnic diversity and social cohesion debate. *European Sociological Review*, 32(1), 54–67; Van Heerden, S., and Ruedin, D. 2017. How attitudes towards immigrants are shaped by residential context: The role of ethnic diversity dynamics and immigrant visibility. *Urban Studies*, Oct. 25. https://doi.org/10.1177/0042098017732692.

15. I argue elsewhere that authoritarian populism, as it is called, is just as much

a problem for the Left as it is for the Right; see Carolan, M. 2020. "They say they don't see color, but maybe they should!" Authoritarian populism and colorblind liberal political culture. *Journal of Peasant Studies, 47*(7), 1445–1469. https://doi.or g/10.1080/03066150.2020.1739654.

16. This finding resonates with the conclusions of other studies—e.g., Lay, J. C. 2017. Adjusting to immigrants in two midwestern communities: Same outcome, different process. *Social Science Quarterly, 98*(5), 1731–1748.

17. Bell, A., Ward, P., Tamal, M. E. H., and Killilea, M. 2019. Assessing recall bias and measurement error in high-frequency social data collection for human-environment research. *Population and Environment, 40*(3), 325–345.

18. Menary, R. 2010. Introduction to the special issue on 4E cognition. *Phenomenology and the Cognitive Sciences, 9*(4), 459–463.

19. Rose, D. C. 2011. *The moral foundation of economic behavior.* New York: Oxford University Press; Shapiro, I. 2012. *The moral foundations of politics.* New Haven, CT: Yale University Press.

20. Haidt, J., and Joseph, C. 2004. Intuitive ethics: How innately prepared intuitions generate culturally variable virtues. *Daedalus, 133*(4), 55–66.

21. Clifford, S., and Jerit, J. 2013. How words do the work of politics: Moral foundations theory and the debate over stem cell research. *Journal of Politics, 75*(3), 659–671; Haidt, J. 2013. *The righteous mind: Why good people are divided by politics and religion.* New York: Random House Digital.

22. Severson, A. W., and Coleman, E. A. 2015. Moral frames and climate change policy attitudes. *Social Science Quarterly, 96*(5), 1277–1290.

23. Kahan, D. M., Jenkins-Smith, H., and Braman, D. 2011. Cultural cognition of scientific consensus. *Journal of Risk Research, 14*(2), 147–174, 150.

24. Kahan, Jenkins-Smith, and Braman, 150.

Chapter 5. Working to Respect Those Who Fed Us

1. O'Brien, P., Kruse, J., and Kruse, P. 2014. Gauging the farm sector's sensitivity to immigration reform via changes in labor costs and availability. World Agricultural Economic and Environmental Services (WAEES) and the American Farm Bureau Federation. www.fb.org/files/AFBF_LaborStudy_Feb2014.pdf.

2. Carolan, M. 2018. *The real cost of cheap food.* 2nd ed. New York: Routledge.

3. A range was negotiated with the owner of the farm—between 30 and 35 pickers—beforehand.

4. Scutti, S. 2018. Strawberries again top 2018's "Dirty Dozen" fruits and veggies. *CNN,* April 10. www.cnn.com/2018/04/10/health/2018-dirty-dozen-fruits-and-veggies-ewg/index.html.

5. The plastic enclosures extend the growing season and increase crop quality.

6. Carroll, R. 2016. Fruits of labor: Sunny California is no paradise for farm workers. *The Guardian*, August 15. www.theguardian.com/us-news/2016/aug/15/california-farms-pick-your-own-fruit-vegetables-working-conditions-jobs.

7. Meuleman, B., and Billiet, J. 2012. Measuring attitudes toward immigration in Europe: The cross-cultural validity of the ESS immigration scales. *Ask. Research & Methods*, 21(1), 5–29.

8. See, e.g., USDA Economic Research Service (www.ers.usda.gov/topics/farm-economy/farm-labor); links to relevant documentaries and video clips (e.g., *American Harvest*, www.youtube.com/watch?v=8nyOH2P6xJY); and news articles (e.g., www.latimes.com/business/la-fi-farmworker-abuse-20170510-story.html).

9. Briñol, P., Petty, R. E., and Wagner, B. C. 2011. Embodied attitude change: A self-validation perspective. *Social and Personality Psychology Compass*, 5(12), 1039–1050.

10. Hammett, D. 2018. Engaging citizens, depoliticizing society? Training citizens as agents for good governance. *Geografiska Annaler: Series B, Human Geography*, 100(2), 64–80. doi:10.1080/04353684.2018.1433961; Isin, E. 2009. Citizenship in flux: The figure of the activist citizen. *Subjectivity 29*, 367–388.

11. Akerlof, K. L., Rowan, K. E., La Porte, T., Batten, B. K., Ernst, H., and Sklarew, D. M. 2016. Risky business: Engaging the public on sea level rise and inundation. *Environmental Science & Policy, 66*, 314–323; Kahan, D. M., Jenkins-Smith, H., and Braman, D. 2011. Cultural cognition of scientific consensus. *Journal of Risk Research, 14*(2), 147–174.

12. Fisher, P. I. 2016. Definitely not moralistic: State political culture and support for Donald Trump in the race for the 2016 Republican presidential nomination. *PS: Political Science & Politics, 49*(4), 743–747; Zanocco, C. M., and Jones, M. D. 2018. Cultural worldviews and political process preferences. *Social Science Quarterly, 99*(4), 1377–1389.

13. See, e.g., Celtic Cross. ADL [Anti-Defamation League website], www.adl.org/education/references/hate-symbols/celtic-cross.

14. Ssemugabo, C., Halage, A. A., Neebye, R. M., Nabankema, V., Kasule, M. M., Ssekimpi, D., and Jørs, E. 2017. Prevalence, circumstances, and management of acute pesticide poisoning in hospitals in Kampala City, Uganda. *Environmental Health Insights, 11*. doi:10.1177/1178630217728924.

15. National Crop Insurance Services: National Survey of Registered Voters Regarding Crop Insurance, April 3–7, 2016. 2016. North Star Opinion Research. www.farmpolicyfacts.org/wp-content/uploads/2016/05/Crop-Insurance-Public-Opinion-Poll.pdf.

16. U.S. Farmers and Ranchers Alliance. 2011. Nationwide surveys reveal disconnect between Americans and their food. Cision PR Newswire, Sept. 22.

www.prnewswire.com/news-releases/nationwide-surveys-reveal-disconnect-between-americans-and-their-food-130336143.html.

17. Gervis, Z. 2019. Here's how many Americans consider themselves "foodies." *New York Post*, May 28. https://nypost.com/2019/05/28/heres-how-many-americans-consider-themselves-foodies.

18. See Godwin, K. R. 2019. Farmer suicide and access to care in Iowa (order no. 13860335). ProQuest Dissertations & Theses Global. (2299502954). https://search.proquest.com/docview/2299502954?accountid=1022.

19. Day, J., and Smith, D. 2016. A glance at the age structure and labor force participation of rural America. *US Census*, Dec 8. www.census.gov/newsroom/blogs/random-samplings/2016/12/a_glance_at_the_age.html.

20. Semuels, A. 2016. The graying of rural America. *The Atlantic*, June 2. www.theatlantic.com/business/archive/2016/06/the-graying-of-rural-america/485159.

21. See, e.g., Open the Books. www.openthebooks.com/map/?Map=6&MapType=Pin.

22. USDA Economic Research Service. 2021. Highlights from the August 2021 Farm Income Forecast. www.ers.usda.gov/topics/farm-economy/farm-sector-income-finances/highlights-from-the-farm-income-forecast.

23. Evich, H. 2017. The vegetable technology gap. *Politico*, March 8. www.politico.com/agenda/story/2017/03/fruits-and-vegtables-technology-000337?platform=hootsuite.

24. CBS News. 2019. Trump farm subsidies: Farmers find ways to boost their payments. *CBS News*, July 3. www.cbsnews.com/news/trump-farm-subsidies-farmers-find-ways-to-boost-their-payments.

25. This specific statistic was retracted shortly thereafter by the CDC for being an overestimation. However, some health care scholars have argued that those original CDC figures are actually an *under*estimation, because (1) the data collected skipped several major agricultural states (like Iowa), and (2) an unknown number of farmers disguise their suicides as farm accidents. See, e.g., Weingarten, D. 2018. Why are America's farmers killing themselves? *The Guardian*, Dec 11. www.theguardian.com/us-news/2017/dec/06/why-are-americas-farmers-killing-themselves-in-record-numbers.

26. Also known as Willing Workers on Organic Farms, in which case the acronym is WWOF.

27. Wiesel, E. 1999. The perils of indifference. https://americanrhetoric.com/speeches/ewieselperilsofindifference.html.

28. See, e.g., Carolan, M. 2018. Justice across real and imagined food worlds: Rural corn growers, urban agriculture activists, and the political ontologies they live by. *Rural Sociology*, 83(4), 823–856; Pilgeram, R. 2012. Social sustainability and

the white, nuclear family: Constructions of gender, race, and class at a Northwest farmers' market. *Race, Gender & Class, 19*(1/2), 37–60.

29. Calo, A. 2016. For farmers, this land is often someone else's. *San Francisco Chronicle*, Oct. 28. www.sfchronicle.com/opinion/article/For-farmers-this-land-is-often-someone-else-s-10420689.php.

30. See, e.g., Anguelovski, I. 2015. Alternative food provision conflicts in cities: Contesting food privilege, injustice, and whiteness in Jamaica Plain, Boston. *Geoforum, 58,* 184–194; and Slocum, R. 2007. Whiteness, space and alternative food practice. *Geoforum, 38*(3), 520–533.

31. USDA Economic Research Service. Farm business income. www.ers.usda.gov/topics/farm-economy/farm-sector-income-finances/farm-business-income.

32. Suneson, G. 2019. What are the 25 lowest paying jobs in the US? Women usually hold them. *USA Today,* June 7. www.usatoday.com/story/money/2019/04/04/25-lowest-paying-jobs-in-us-2019-includes-cooking-cleaning/39264277.

33. FCC. n.d. Bridging the digital divide for all Americans. Federal Communications Commission. www.fcc.gov/about-fcc/fcc-initiatives/bridging-digital-divide-all-americans.

Chapter 6. Urban-Rural Food Plans

1. Ufheil, A. 2020. How poor broadband access is hurting Colorado's rural communities during COVID-19. *5280: Denver's Mile High Magazine*, Sept. www.5280.com/2020/09/how-poor-broadband-access-is-hurting-colorados-rural-communities-during-covid-19.

2. United States Census Bureau. 2016. New census data show differences between urban and rural populations. www.census.gov/newsroom/press-releases/2016/cb16-210.html.

3. Feyerabend, P. 2001. *Conquest of abundance: A tale of abstraction versus the richness of being.* Chicago: University of Chicago Press, 3–4.

4. For a map of these counties, see, e.g., Colorado Health Center. 2016. Colorado: County Designations, 2016. www.colorado.gov/pacific/sites/default/files/PCO_CHSC_CountyDesignations_2016.pdf.

5. Carolan, M. 2019. Filtering perceptions of climate change and biotechnology: Values and views among Colorado farmers and ranchers. *Climatic Change, 159,* 121–139. doi.org/10.1007/s10584-019-02625-0.

6. Miller, M. 2019. King of the road: Breaking down the popularity of pickup trucks. *Experian*, August 30. www.experian.com/blogs/insights/2019/08/king-road-breaking-popularity-pickup-trucks.

7. Carolan, Filtering perceptions of climate change (see note 5 above);

Darnhofer, I., Lamine, C., Strauss, A., and Navarrete, M. 2016. The resilience of family farms: Towards a relational approach. *Journal of Rural Studies, 44*, 111–122; Realo, A., Allik, J., and Vadi, M. 1997. The hierarchical structure of collectivism. *Journal of Research in Personality, 31*(1), 93–116.

8. Kelly, K. 2009. The new socialism: Global collectivist society is coming online. *Wired Magazine*, www.wired.com/2009/05/nep-newsocialism; Lilley, K., Barker, M., and Harris, N. 2015. Exploring the process of global citizen learning and the student mind-set. *Journal of Studies in International Education, 19*(3), 225–245.

9. Enos, R. 2017. *The space between us: Social geography and politics.* New York: Cambridge University Press.

10. Quoted in Florida, R. 2017. How place shapes our politics. Bloomberg CityLab, Dec. 12. www.citylab.com/life/2017/12/how-place-shapes-our-politics/548147.

11. Enos. *The space between us.*

12. Quoted in Florida, How place shapes our politics.

13. See, e.g., Milan Urban Food Policy Pack. n.d. Local solutions for global issues. www.milanurbanfoodpolicypact.org.

14. Horchy, E. 2020. New Port Richey joins global food sustainability initiative. *Suncoast News*, July 22. www.suncoastnews.com/news/new-port-richey-joins-global-food-sustainability-initiative/article_bcf38f70-cc5f-11ea-88d2-17892e73a633.html.

15. Cabannes, Y., and Marocchino, C. (Eds.). 2018. *Integrating food into urban planning.* London: UCL Press.

16. Denver City Council et al. 2017. Denver Food Vision. www.denvergov.org/content/dam/denvergov/Portals/771/documents/CH/Final_FoodVision_120717.pdf.

17. Department of Public Health and Environment. 2015. Childhood overweight and obesity in Colorado. www.colorado.gov/pacific/sites/default/files/DC_fact-sheet_slides_Childhood-Obesity_August_2015.pdf.

18. Center for Good Food Purchasing. n.d. https://goodfoodpurchasing.org/program-overview.

19. Sayer, A. 2005. Class, moral worth and recognition. *Sociology, 39*(5), 947–963, 961.

20. A Google search indicates this quote came from Philip Stanhope, Fourth Earl of Chesterfield (1695–1773).

21. Rivera, L. A., and Tilcsik, A. 2016. Class advantage, commitment penalty: The gendered effect of social class signals in an elite labor market. *American Sociological Review, 81*(6), 1097–1131.

22. Campbell, H., Bell, M. M., and Finney, M. 2006. *Country boys: Masculinity*

and rural life. University Station: Pennsylvania State University Press; Laoire, C. N. 1999. Gender issues in Irish rural outmigration. In P. Boyle and K. Halfacree (Eds.), *Migration and gender in the developed world* (pp. 223–237). London: Routledge; Laoire, C. N. 2001. A matter of life and death? Men, masculinities and staying "behind" in rural Ireland. *Sociologia Ruralis, 41*(2), 220–236; Laoire, C. N. 2005. "You're not a man at all": Masculinity, responsibility and staying on the land in contemporary Ireland." *Irish Journal of Sociology, 14*(2), 94–114.

23. Rossier, R. 2005. Role models and farm development options: A comparison of seven Swiss farm families. *Journal of Comparative Family Studies, 36*(3), 399–417.

24. Carolan, M. 2019. The rural problem: Justice in the countryside. *Rural Sociology,* May 9. https://doi.org/10.1111/ruso.12278.

25. Chait, J. 2019. Largest organic retailers in North America. *The Balance,* Nov 20. www.thebalancesmb.com/organic-retailers-in-north-america-2011-2538129.

26. Guthman, J. 2003. Fast food/organic food: Reflexive tastes and the making of "yuppie chow." *Social and Cultural Geography, 4*(1): 45–58, 45.

27. Simpson, K. 2017. Colorado divide: Seismic shifts create rural-urban chasm in the culture, economy and politics of the state. *Denver Post,* July 21. www.denverpost.com/2017/07/21/colorado-divide-rural-urban-chasm.

28. Finlay, L. 2006. Dancing between embodied empathy and phenomenological reflection. *Indo-Pacific Journal of Phenomenology, 6,* supp. 1, 1–11, 2. doi:10.1080/20797222.2006.11433930.

29. Stein, E. 1989 [1916]. *On the problem of empathy.* 3rd ed. W. Stein, trans. (p. 10). Washington, DC: ICS.

Chapter 7. Forest to Table

1. See, e.g., Carolan, M. 2019/2020. Automated agrifood futures: Robotics, labor and the distributive politics of digital agriculture. *Journal of Peasant Studies, 47*(1), 184–207. https://doi.org/10.1080/03066150.2019.1584189.

2. See, e.g., Salter, J. 2020. St. Louis couple indicted for waving guns at protesters. Associated Press, Oct 6. https://apnews.com/article/st-louis-indictments-racial-injustice-3bbed2ea6c982581e51b16123a785cfc.

3. Parker, K., Horowitz, J. M., Igielnik, R., Oliphant, J. B., and Brown, A. 2017. The demographics of gun ownership. Pew Research Center, June 22. www.pewsocialtrends.org/2017/06/22/the-demographics-of-gun-ownership.

4. Igielnik, R. 2017. Rural and urban gun owners have different experiences, views on gun policy. Pew Research Center, July 10. www.pewresearch.org/fact-tank/2017/07/10/rural-and-urban-gun-owners-have-different-experiences-views-on-gun-policy.

5. See, e.g., Butler, J. 2011. *Gender trouble: Feminism and the subversion of identity*. New York: Routledge.

6. Clark, A., and Chalmers, D. 1998. The extended mind. *Analysis, 58*(1), 7–19. https://doi.org/10.1111/1467-8284.00096.

7. Clark, A. 1999a. Where brain, body, and world collide. *Journal of Cognitive Systems Research, 1*(1), 5–17; Clark, A. 1999b. *Being there: Putting brain, body and the world together again*. Cambridge, MA: MIT Press.

8. Levinas, E. 1969. *Totality and infinity: An essay on exteriority*. Pittsburgh: Duquesne University Press.

9. Yi, J., Todd, N. R., and Mekawi, Y. 2020. Racial colorblindness and confidence in and likelihood of action to address prejudice. *American Journal of Community Psychology, 65*(3–4), 407–422.

10. See Ross, J. 2015. Obama revives his "cling to guns or religion" analysis—for Donald Trump supporters. *Washington Post*, Dec 21. www.washingtonpost.com/news/the-fix/wp/2015/12/21/obama-dusts-off-his-cling-to-guns-or-religion-idea-for-donald-trump.

11. See, e.g., Beeman, A. 2015. Walk the walk but don't talk the talk: The strategic use of color-blind ideology in an interracial social movement organization. *Sociological Forum, 30*(1), 127–147; Herring, C., Keith, V., and Horton, H. D. 2004. *Skin deep: How race and complexion matter in the "color-blind" era*. Champaign: University of Illinois Press.

12. This point was recently corroborated in Evan Mandery's excellent piece in the October 13, 2019, issue of *Politico*: What teaching ethics in Appalachia taught me about bridging America's partisan divide. www.politico.com/magazine/story/2019/10/13/america-cultural-divide-red-state-blue-state-228111.

13. Barrett, M. 2020. Trump criticizes Whitmer after FBI foiled plot to kidnap Michigan governor. *Michigan Live*, Oct. 8. www.mlive.com/public-interest/2020/10/trump-criticizes-whitmer-after-fbi-foiled-plot-to-kidnap-michigan-governor.html.

14. McLuhan, M. 1964. *Understanding media: The extensions of man*. New York: McGraw Hill.

15. My wife and kids were visiting grandparents in Chicago, which is why I had the house to myself and why they are not present in this story.

16. Stroud, A. 2012. Good guys with guns: Hegemonic masculinity and concealed handguns. *Gender & Society, 26*(2), 216–238.

Chapter 8. Final Thoughts and New Trajectories

1. Doris, J. *Lack of character: Personality and moral behavior*. New York: Cambridge University Press, 168.

2. Nussbaum, M. C. 2016. *Anger and forgiveness: Resentment, generosity, judgment.* New York: Oxford University Press, 125.

3. Nussbaum, 96.

4. Quoted in Popova, M. 2015. A rap on race: Margaret Mead and James Baldwin's rare conversation on forgiveness and the difference between guilt and responsibility. *Brain Pickings*, March 19. www.brainpickings.org/2015/03/19/a-rap-on-race-margaret-mead-and-james-baldwin.

5. Ehrenreich, B. 2001. *Nickel and dimed: On (not) getting by in America.* New York: Holt.

6. Salmond, J. A. 1967. *The Civilian Conservation Corps, 1933–1942: A New Deal case study.* National Park Service, Washington, DC. www.nps.gov/parkhistory/online_books/ccc/salmond/contents.htm.

7. Quotes from Chappell, B. 2019. Should young Americans be required to do public service? Federal panel says maybe. *NPR*, Jan 23. www.npr.org/2019/01/23/687715869/should-young-americans-be-required-to-do-public-service-federal-panel-says-maybe.

8. Carolan, M. 2021. COVID-19's impact on gendered household food practices: Eating and feeding as expressions of competencies, moralities, and mobilities. *Sociological Quarterly.* https://doi.org/10.1080/00380253.2020.1870415.

9. Cho, H., Li, W., Cannon, J., Lopez, R., and Song, C. 2020. Testing three explanations for stigmatization of people of Asian descent during COVID-19: Maladaptive coping, biased media use, or racial prejudice? *Ethnicity & Health*, 1–16; Cinone, D. 2020. "SHAME ON HIM": Florida Gov. Ron DeSantis blames coronavirus rise on "overwhelmingly Hispanic" workers. *The Sun*, June 19. www.the-sun.com/news/1008235/florida-governor-desantis-blames-coronavirus-rise-hispanic-workers.

10. Nail, P. R., McGregor, I., Drinkwater, A. E., Steele, G. M., and Thompson, A. W. 2009. Threat causes liberals to think like conservatives. *Journal of Experimental Social Psychology, 45*(4), 901–907; Robson, D. 2020. The fear of coronavirus is changing our psychology. *BBC*, April 1. www.bbc.com/future/article/20200401-covid-19-how-fear-of-coronavirus-is-changing-our-psychology.

11. Huang, J. Y., Sedlovskaya, A., Ackerman, J. M., and Bargh, J. A. 2011. Immunizing against prejudice: Effects of disease protection on attitudes toward out-groups. *Psychological Science, 22*(12), 1550–1556.

12. Napier, J. L., Huang, J., Vonasch, A. J., and Bargh, J. A. 2018. Superheroes for change: Physical safety promotes socially (but not economically) progressive attitudes among conservatives. *European Journal of Social Psychology, 48*(2), 187–195.

13. Stewart, J. 2020. It's a "swimming naked" moment: The financial system has a real test. *New York Times*, March 10. www.nytimes.com/2020/03/10/business/stock-market-coronavirus-crisis.html.

14. Hume, D. 1777/2004. *An enquiry concerning the principles of morals.* Amherst, NY: Prometheus; Smith, A. 1790/2006. *The theory of moral sentiments.* Mineola, NY: Dover.

15. Coplan, A., and Goldie, P. 2011. Introduction. In A. Coplan and P. Goldie (Eds.), *Empathy: Philosophical and psychological perspectives* (pp. ix–xlvii, ix). Oxford: Oxford University Press.

16. Pedwell, C. 2016. De-colonising empathy: Thinking affect transnationally. *Samyukta: A Journal of Women's Studies, 16*(1), 27–49, 40 (emphasis in original).

17. See the discussion of this term at https://twitter.com/natesilver538/status/1 205893784963297282?lang=en.

18. Phelps, J. 2020. Trump defends 2017 "very fine people" comments, calls Robert E. Lee "a great general." ABC News, April 26. https://abcnews. go.com/Politics/trump-defends-2017-fine-people-comments-calls-robert/ story?id=62653478.

Index

Lightning Source UK Ltd.
Milton Keynes UK
UKHW012106150921
390638UK00003B/35/J